Confronting Death
Psychoreligious Responses

Studies in Religion, No. 4

Margaret R. Miles, Series Editor

Professor of Historical Theology
The Divinity School
Harvard University

Other Titles in This Series

Confronting Death
Psychoreligious Responses

by
Ralph C. Johnston, Jr.

UMI Research Press

Ann Arbor / London

Produced and distributed by
UMI Research Press
an imprint of
University Microfilms Inc.
Ann Arbor, Michigan 48106

Library of Congress Cataloging in Publication Data

Johnston, Ralph C. (Ralph Clovis), 1947-
  Confronting death : psychoreligious responses / by Ralph
C. Johnston, Jr.
    p. cm—(Studies in religion ; no. 4)
    Bibliography: p.
    Includes index.
    ISBN 0-8357-1795-X (alk. paper)
    1. Death—Religious aspects—Christianity   2. Death—
Psychological aspects   I. Title.   II. Series: Studies in religion
(Ann Arbor, Mich.) ; no. 4.
  BT825.J64   1988
  155.9'37—dc19   88-25108
                                                              CIP

British Library CIP data is available.

For
Team Two Crisis Counselors
GMHC, Inc., New York City

Ralph Clovis Johnston, Jr. touched all of those with whom he came in contact, and his desire to live life to its fullest became a model for others to follow. As his brother, I was fortunate to witness not only the way he approached life but also the way he wrestled with and came to terms with dying. This book is a way for Ralph to continue to help others as they, too, struggle to make sense of the mystery of death.

Lon Ben Johnston

Contents

Foreword

It has often been said that death is our society's last great taboo. A few generations ago, death and mourning were familiar household events; in the same bed where children were born, their parents died. Ronald Blythe expresses this unforgettably in an introduction to Tolstoy's *The Death of Ivan Ilyich*:

> Where first and last cries were heard in the very same room, where the first things looked at were often the last things seen, where the corpse lay where the lover's body moved, when the entire intimacy of life from start to finish was confined to the family house and not to maternity wings, terminal wards and funeral parlors, death itself possessed dimensions and connotations that are now either forgotten or stifled. Everyone until recently knew the actual smell of death.

If our Victorian grandparents and great-grandparents were intimate with mortality, they also had the consolation of a religious worldview that promised a life beyond death. In the first half of the nineteenth century, the rural cemetery movement and the cozy, sentimental depictions of death in popular fiction contributed to a domestic and pastoral image of death, while pious intellectuals worked to defend the hope of survival against the inroads of scientific materialism. The second half of the nineteenth century and the first half of the twentieth were marked by increasing sentimentalization of death in some circles (notably, the spiritualist movement) and increasing death anxiety in others, leading psychologists from Freud to Becker to Lifton to conclude that modern society is built upon denial of death and driven by the dread that our stratagems to deny death might fail. Death signals the failure of our medical technology, the evaporation of our dream of progress, the ultimate thwarting of the individual's quest for self-fulfillment. No wonder that we must deny death.

How paradoxical, then, that recent years have seen an apparent reversal of the death taboo. Books on death and dying (or, in New Age jargon, deathing) compete for room on the bestseller lists with books on dieting and dressing for success. Is it possible that the beautiful death—which seemed an untenably quaint notion in the wake of World War II, with its horrific manifestations of mass death—is making a comeback? There is no simple answer to this question. Contemporary attitudes toward death are characterized by ambivalence and puzzling contradictions; one needs a competent guide to negotiate this peculiar and sometimes treacherous landscape.

Ralph Johnston is such a guide. From a remarkably unbiased standpoint, he sorts out the major alternative ways of viewing death in our culture, and offers the reader an opportunity to assimilate what seems most valid from a dizzying array of choices. Johnston succinctly explains the work of such challenging writers on death as Philippe Ariès, Ernest Becker, and Robert Jay Lifton, and introduces the reader to those disciplines that have a bearing on our understanding of death: psychology (in its analytical, depth, transpersonal, and behavioral schools), philosophy (both humanistic and existentialist), sociology, social anthropology, and, of course, theology.

Johnston's thesis is that our failure to come to terms with death can be corrected only by overcoming the isolation of the contemporary family and individual, the egoism and narcissism of our individualistic culture, and the loss of connection we feel to ancestors and posterity, to sacred tradition, and to the cosmos. The thanatology movement has tried to remedy our culture's pervasive denial of death by a campaign of consciousness-raising. Admirable as this is, Johnston argues, the death-and-dying movement unwittingly serves the demon of narcissism by portraying death as a blissful and transformative experience.

Johnston's discussion is more than a critique of the thanatology movement; he takes on a whole range of spiritually-oriented psychotherapies, with which he is sympathetic in many respects, but which he justly criticizes for being captive to the values of the me-generation, insufficiently aware of history, and inadequate as a basis for the creation of community. His allegiance lies with Robert Jay Lifton and, indirectly, Erik Erikson, rather than with the many similar-sounding New Age psychoreligions. He also aligns himself with Jacob Needleman in calling for a recovery of sacred tradition. With this idea in mind, he turns to the writings of Christian theologians, joining with those who advocate a theology of the darkness of death, in which death is neither denied nor easily rehabilitated. Death retains its sting; suffering is real; but transformation is possible through transcendence of the self and identification with the wider community and cosmos.

Johnston's work is one more sign of the maturing of Christian theological discourse about death. More importantly, this is not just a book about death, but also about our society's urgent need for an authentic spirituality. Johnston points out that the new psychologists have, so to speak, cannibalized the religious traditions in their search for spiritual techniques and peak experiences. His effort is to reclaim some of the popular hunger for sacred experience, and to find a place for this searching within the Christian tradition. It is a worthy enterprise, and one that deserves the collaboration of many serious thinkers.

Carol Zaleski

1

Introduction

"Men are subject to death, misery and ignorance, and, as they know no cure, they refuse to think of them."[1] Pascal's seventeenth-century observation, particularly with regard to death, has been remarkably true of twentieth-century Western societies. With the decline of religious belief and the ascendency of technology, the company of the dying has become increasingly intolerable. We have preferred to exclude the dying from our homes (commending them instead to the care of strangers) and to banish death as a subject of conversation or of investigation, because it implies the inevitability of our own.

The appearance of Gorer's "The Pornography of Death" in 1955[2] broke this taboo and seemed to release a flood of publication that was in full flow by 1963. Within the last two decades the subject has been approached from every conceivable angle and throughout the spectrum of academic disciplines—psychological, sociological, theological, anthropological, legal, medical, historical, and literary.[3] American popular culture too, and to a lesser extent that of Europe, has exhibited a fascination with death: in 1976, The New York Times Book Review listed two surprising bestsellers—Raymond A. Moody's Life after Life and Elisabeth Kübler-Ross's On Death and Dying[4] (the latter has become something of a classic among academic "thanatologists"). Given the strength of the taboo, this was an astonishing development.

The surge of interest in death and dying has been accompanied, indeed characterized by, proliferating therapies and strategies whose aim is to lessen our horror of death and to reintegrate the dying into the community of the living. At the same time, the abrupt emergence of the thanatology movement poses questions whose answers may be

Publisher's note: Ralph C. Johnston, Jr. was unable to complete revisions of the manuscript of Confronting Death: Psychoreligious Responses before his death. The final text has been prepared with the editorial assistance of Sarah Jeffries and Walter Michener.

essential to its success. First, what is it that has provoked this sudden violation of one of our culture's most implacable taboos, allowing death to leap from the obituary column to the bestseller list? Second, can the strategies on which the death-and-dying movement is founded succeed in fostering acceptance and understanding of death, in reestablishing it as part of life?

In attempting to understand the context out of which the thanatology movement has so unexpectedly sprung, the work of French thinker Philippe Ariès is critical. In his panoramic study of historical attitudes toward dying, *The Hour of Our Death*,[5] Ariès casts light on the emergence of the idea of death as terrifying and (literally) unspeakable that has characterized contemporary Western society, and to which the thanatology movement is a reaction.

Ariès's survey of the last fifteen hundred years of European society distinguishes among five cultural models of death. (He does not suggest that these constitute a simple evolutionary sequence; rather the five variations comprise a series of overlapping and often coinciding images, which conform only broadly to a long-term chronological development.) Of these, we are particularly interested in the most ancient and the most recent.

The first attitude toward death he discerns is, according to Ariès, typical of most primitive societies. In this conception, the living and the dead are in total harmony, and death's inevitability is accepted without fear. This attitude gained special force in Europe, where the early Christian concept of death reinforced the fundamental vision,[6] and, indeed, it remained the dominant one for the majority of European society well into the nineteenth century, particularly in peasant communities such as those described by Tolstoy. Death was accepted as a kind of extended sleep in which one awaited the body's ultimate resurrection in time for the Last Judgment, and society had complete trust in the Church's ability to look after the interests of the souls of the departed. Ariès has termed this familiar and nonhorrific image the "tame" death.[7]

This cultural idea of a "tame," nonthreatening death first began to change during the eleventh and twelfth centuries among the social and intellectual elite, whose wealth and status led them to exalt the individual, who increasingly took precedence over the community. Amid a growing emphasis on personal destiny both in life and after death, collective commemorations for the dead lost ground to requiem masses for individuals, and symbolic emphasis shifted from the deathbed to the funeral, which became an increasingly ostentatious display of status and wealth.[8]

The Enlightenment of the eighteenth century saw the beginnings of a deep faith in progress and in the inevitable triumph of science over nature. Death somehow could not fit into this vision and Enlightened European society became increasingly ill-at-ease with the one condition it could never cure. Simultaneously, the demands of health reformers that cemeteries be relocated away from churches and city centers constituted a powerful symbolic rejection of the dead from the community of the living. Death seemed to have little place in this brave new world and as such was both unreal and frightening.

These trends away from the "tame" death have culminated in the twentieth century in a cultural model of death as something "wild," too frightening to be spoken of, looked at, or thought about. Consequently we have created what Ariès calls "hidden" or "invisible" death. The privacy that had already come to surround death intensified. Death has been taken out of the home and placed in the hospital, where strangers are paid to do the nursing formerly performed by the family.[9] In 1949, only about 50 percent of deaths in the United States occurred in hospitals. By the mid-1980s, this figure is thought to have risen as high as 80 percent.[10] In addition, those who die in hospitals are likely to be kept under heavy sedation toward the end; dying has become a process in which not even the dying person consciously participates.

It is difficult to argue with Ariès's general proposition that humanity's relationship to nature, and hence to death, has become increasingly distorted as our society has become increasingly technological. Marion Levy has suggested that modernization may be defined as the growing proportion of inanimate as opposed to animate sources of power.[11] Overwhelmingly, inanimate technology is characteristic of our age, and it has profoundly altered the way we think about our existence. In addition, scientific discoveries about the size and age of the universe have significant and often demoralizing implications for the place of humanity within it, and what is done with those implications goes beyond the responsibilities of science. Arnold Toynbee has noted that the progress of scientific knowledge in the West has resulted in the reduction of humanity's position to "apparent insignificance in both the space-dimension and the time-dimension."[12]

Thus the transformation of death into a terrifying spectre is due in part to the modern threat to the plausibility of theodicies. Modernity has not, however, managed to do away with the experiences, such as death, that made these theodicies necessary in the first place. The great world religions and the beliefs of most surviving nontechnological peoples provide explanations for the fate of the individual after death.

These beliefs make dying easier to bear. Recently, in Western societies, the erosion of belief in an afterlife that has accompanied the adoption of the scientific world-view has removed this source of comfort. As we shall see, the response of Christian theologians themselves to the conundrums posed by scientific thought has been mixed,[13] but Christian theology must accept some responsibility for the emergence of the "wild" death.

But if the scientific world-view has, since the eighteenth century, increasingly replaced the religious one as a model for understanding the universe, it too seems endangered by a growing disillusionment with technology. The psychologist/philosopher Jacob Needleman has decribed contemporary Western civilization as existing "between two dreams."[14] The dream from which we are awakening was the one in which our technological culture was born, that of the rationalism and idealism of the eighteenth and nineteenth centuries. In this vision, human progress was to be founded on the scientific method, and observations and experiments were the path that would lead to salvation through reason and technology. Science was to be mankind's servant and friend, set to work bettering the material conditions of life.

This dream has begun to fragment with the gradual realization that the discoveries of modern science, technology, and even medicine have not come without damaging effects, physical, psychological, and spiritual. Furthermore, science has lost much of its credibility as a means of improving life because of the ecological crisis, the threat of nuclear war, and the disruption of our life patterns by advanced technologies. Increasingly, science, once the foundation of a wonderful dream of the human future, has become the object of mistrust and disappointment.

Behind Needleman's second dream, a dream of "inward progress," is the desire, still largely inchoate, to humanize the juggernaut of technology. This dream is based on the hope that humanity can rectify the moral and psychological flaws which have corrupted the technological vision and produced scientific creations that are both alienating and destructive. Thus, in Needleman's view, with the vision of a scientific utopia rapidly dissipating and the idea of "inward progress" still largely at the stage of hopeful thinking, we are living between dreams. The earlier dream, while displacing religion as a source of universal context, has resulted in a world-view in which we have been reluctant to address such questions as the meaning of death. The result, of course, is that when that mortality looms, we are unable to come to terms with it. Death, which once was "tame," has become "wild."

The increasingly technological orientation of Western culture is not the only trend that Ariès perceives as responsible for transforming death from "tame" to "wild." Another corresponding process has been the changing relationship of the individual to society. Modern thought about death has been shaped profoundly by the rising sense of the importance of individuality and the concomitant decline in the role of the community. The "tame" death was (and in parts of the world still is) characteristic of small, closely knit communities. In modern urban society, most of us find little sense of community in the abstractions of our nationalities or religious affiliations. Beyond this vague allegiance to some such great collectivity, we have little feeling, in our increasingly urban and impersonal society, of attachment to more than a few other individuals, who may or may not be family members. It is within this limited sphere that most of us find fulfillment, if we find it at all.

Given this sort of radical individualism, "it is no accident," writes Robert Hendin, "that at the present time the dominant events in psychoanalysis are the rediscovery of narcissism and the new emphasis on the psychological significance of death."[15] Other critics have described our entire culture as narcissistic, a term referring, in psychoanalytic terms, to a disorder characterized by a facility in managing the impressions one gives to others, a hunger for admiration accompanied by contempt for those manipulated into providing it, and a terror of aging and death. As Ivan Illych has suggested, "a society's image of death reveals the level of independence of its people, their personal relatedness, self-reliance, and aliveness."[16]

Ethicist Daniel Callahan of the Hudson Institute has described the contemporary "mixture of individualism and technological *hubris*" as "about as dangerous a mix as can be imagined."[17] The result of this volatile blend has been a "tyranny of survival"—a radical denial of death that manifests itself in a cultural taboo on discussion of or confrontation with our mortality.

How, then, can we explain the birth of the thanatology movement, a violation of one of our culture's most rigid proscriptions? Certainly, the crumbling dream of scientific salvation has left us with a conception of death more frightening, more "wild" than ever before. Increasingly, death is characterized by physical violence, whether from the invasive techniques of contemporary medical care, or from the growing likelihood of being a victim of crime, nationalism, or nuclearism. It has been argued that the very language formerly used to speak of death has become inaccessible to us as a consequence of the mass exterminations of the holocaust and the horrific destruction at Hiroshima and Nagasaki.

Nuclear technology, at least insofar as it involves weapons, undeniably affects contemporary attitudes toward death. Michael Carey interviewed more than forty people who grew up during the Red Scare and the bombshelter-building era. As it became apparent that nuclear war would perhaps be postponed, the bombshelters became clubhouses for adolescents, and anxiety appeared to fade, but Carey found that as adults many of these people report a vague but insistent sense of living in the shadow of the bomb, and a feeling that their own lives, or those of their children, will end violently and prematurely.

As Ivan Illych observes, for the first time in history, "instead of being due to the will of God, or man's guilt, or the laws of nature, Armageddon has become a possible consequence of man's direct decision."[18] Under the circumstances it is hardly surprising that our attitudes toward death are again ready to undergo some sort of metamorphosis. It is an inevitable consequence of what Robert Jay Lifton refers to as "our present preoccupation with absurd death (and, by implication, absurd life) and unlimited technological violence."[19] Lifton contrasts the concept of nuclear extermination with the traditional images of death as a part of life, as the end of life, or as a challenge or a muse.[20] We now equate death with annihilation, and individual death cannot be separated from the death of the entire world.[21] The result is, in Lifton's phrase, a "broken connection" between life and death. In the face of annihilation, the conventional modes of interpreting death—biological, theological, transcendental, natural, and so forth—are rendered absurd.[22]

The thanatology movement seems to have arisen in response to this latest permutation in our culture's tortured relationship with death. The French historian Michel Vovelle has noted that the increasingly violent representations of death in our society have been accompanied by a recurrent nostalgia, in books, films, and theater for the "tame" death that we have lost.[23] Noteworthy are the childlike regression of Ingmar Bergman's Cries and Whispers, and published interviews with the dying, such as those dramatized in Michael Christopher's play, The Shadow Box, which provides a cathartic entry into the world of the dying person. Indeed Ariès's work itself represents a plea for a return to a world in which sacred tradition and community values deprive death of its terror.

A culture's image of death has been called "a primary symbolic medium for collective consciousness issues."[24] The predominant images of death today—nuclear annihilation; the death of the patient in the hospital, covered with tubes—suggest that our collective consciousness is terrorized. The death-and-dying movement seeks to free our society of the spectre of the "wild" death, to make death an issue that can be talked about, confronted, and, finally, accepted as part of life. It has been suggested that thanatology has become a "new theology" for a generation in which the traditional symbols surrounding death have become bankrupt,[25] either powerless or harmful. This book is an examination of the premises of this "new theology."

Much of the recent intellectual flurry surrounding death has occurred in various branches of the social sciences, in particular psychology and sociology, and most contemporary thanatologies derive from various psychotherapies. The terminal patient in a modern hospital who wants to talk about death is often referred to a psychologist or a social worker rather than a chaplain. In any case, the chaplain, if there is one, will more than likely have been trained in the same traditions of clinical psychology as the others.

Yet the psychotherapeutic enterprise as a whole has been criticized by sociologist Philip Rieff as a manifestation of precisely that radical individualism implicated in the creation of "hidden" and "wild" death. Rieff sees this individualism as the most serious malady of our culture, which has become one in which every member believes that he or she can and must have everything desired, including a good or appropriate death.[26] In his view, the "triumph of the therapeutic" (similar to Needleman's dream of "inward progress") is in actuality a tyranny of individualism. The aim of the "therapeutic" is the realization of well-being through the healing of wounds suffered as a result of the constraints of society. In Rieff's view, the ultimate goal of psychoanalysis is a liberation of the self from others. This freedom from the community is achieved through "the therapeutic approach to life, substituting analysis for ideals, theory for belief, detachment for commitment, and coolness for ardor."[27]

If the "turn inward" of Needleman's second dream and of most thanatologies is to be a turn in the right direction, it will require a complementary social ethic. We need a therapy that stresses a commitment to community as a balance to individual freedom. It is precisely this sort of ethic that is lacking in those segments of the thanatology movement that focus primarily on the needs of the individual. But as Daniel Callahan points out, both the tyranny of individualism and the tryanny of survival "are proof against any kind of social ethic, for both dissolve that necessary dialectic between individual and community which is the prime requirement for such an ethic."[28]

Naturally, much of the promise offered by the thanatology movement lies in its potential to enhance self-awareness, particularly as it can help to articulate the connectedness of life and death. But if, as Rieff and others have suggested, the "therapeutic approach" is guilty of complicity in the emergence of a narcissistic society, can the thanatology movement, firmly rooted in the human potentials movement and the various psychotherapies it has spawned, escape the same criticisms? If Western society's current inability to cope with the concept of death has arisen in response to the glorification of the individual at the expense of the community, is the answer to the problem likely to be found in approaches founded on the same principle?

2

The Thanatology Movement: Attitudes and Values

The thanatology movement, which has emerged in its popular form since the publication of Kübler-Ross's *On Death and Dying* in 1969, can only be called a movement in the broadest sense. Referred to variously as the "natural death movement," the "death with dignity movement," or the "death awareness movement," it embraces a highly diverse collection of organizations and individuals—psychologists, sociologists, physicians, philosophers, and theologians—many of whom may have little sense of being part of anything so organized as a movement. Nonetheless, the subject of death has generated such widespread popular and academic interest recently and provoked such a volume of publication that it is convenient to refer to the phenomenon as a movement, and I have chosen the term "thanatology movement" as perhaps the most inclusive. Despite the evident diversity of opinions and approaches among thanatologists, there are common threads. If we can ascertain the general goals of thanatologists and thanatological institutions, the changes they seek to bring about in our culture's response to death, then we can hope for some insights into the ideologies that, beneath the surface, link the highly disparate components of the movement.

The activities of thanatological organizations fall roughly into two categories. There are, first of all, organizations that seek reform through education, whose goal is to change the way we as a society think of death and the way we interact with the dying. Second, there are also organizations whose approach involves working immediately with the dying and their families.

Among the individuals and organizations devoted to educating, it is a given that since our culture's current difficulties in dealing with death are linked to our refusal to talk about it, then talking about death is just what we need to do. Kübler-Ross's groundbreaking interdisciplinary seminars on death and dying in Chicago in 1965 are an excellent example of discourse as therapy. These meetings, in which students interviewed dying patients, proved therapeutic both for the dying and for the students. The terminal patients quickly overcame their initial shyness and shared their immense loneliness. Writes Kübler-Ross, "Strangers whom we had never met shared their grief, their isolation, their inability to talk about their illness and death with their next-of-kin."[1] The students, in turn, through this contact, became "aware of the necessity of considering death as a real possibility for themselves." The sessions proved "a sort of group therapy with frank confrontations, mutual support, and painful discoveries and insights."[2] Kübler-Ross believes that talking with an empathetic listener can help a dying person work through the difficult preliminary psychological stages to arrive at a peaceful acceptance of death.

An example of another approach to talking as a means of coming to grips with death is that of groups like Compassionate Friends, an organization of parents who have experienced the death of a child. Each meeting begins with an affirmation of personal tragedies in the style of Alcoholics Anonymous and lasts as long as the members feel the urge to share their feelings and think they can provide mutual support. Knowing that their listeners understand, the bereaved parents can find some relief in expressing their pain and bitterness. On the same principle, some communities have established telephone hotlines for the dying or their families. Counseling the dying and their families is increasingly an occupational specialty for psychologists, psychiatrists, priests, ministers, and rabbis, and paperback racks now feature how-to books for the moribund and their loved ones.

Nor does the thanatology movement concentrate exclusively on helping the dying and their families. Many programs have been organized to educate the population at large, on the assumption that the fear of death is not a problem limited to the dying. In the view of many thanatologists, an intellectual and emotional acceptance of death is inextricably linked to full appreciation of life, whether one is in immediate contact with death or not. The existential philosopher/psychologist, Peter Koestenbaum, writes,

> Confronting one's own death, facing up to it, owning up to it, accepting it, integrating it fully into one's experience—all of these psychological realities give us the fullness and richness of the experience of life. The tragic and unfortunate circumstances of death nevertheless give us—vicariously for those who do not confront

their own death but only read how others do it—a genuine appreciation for the beauty and the sanctity of life.[3]

This is just the message being taught in countless books, in national and regional workshops, symposia, and conferences, in community forums, and in colleges, high schools, and even elementary schools. For younger children this may involve visiting cemeteries or talking openly about how they felt when a pet died. Older students may study practical but generally avoided issues like wills, insurance, and care for the dying. A senior high school sociology class in Florida visited a funeral home to observe both the body of an elderly man and the 1,800-degree cremation chamber. Students in college psychology courses are increasingly encouraged to break down the taboo on the subject by talking freely about their own experiences with death and the dying.

The thanatology movement, then, encourages discourse about death both as therapy for the dying and their families and as a means of enabling everyone to derive the maximum satisfaction from life, to develop a sense of purpose and fulfillment. Death education is aimed at both the dying and the living, as a means of enhancing values, relationships, and the quality of the world we build around us. In the words of psychologist Herman Feifel, "Death makes an authentic statement about life's actuality and meaning. Herein lies the summons to advance our comprehension of how death can serve life ... to live decently and die well—this is man's privilege."[4]

Other thanatological organizations are concerned with changing the actual physical circumstances in which we die. Much of this activity arises from a profound dissatisfaction with the overwhelming dominance of medical professionals in what many feel should be a family affair. Most people currently die in hospitals under conditions prescribed by medical practices, beliefs, and bureaucracies, and these conditions may be entirely inappropriate for the dying and their families, becoming a source of torment rather than relief.[5] Critics argue, convincingly, that the emphasis on "curing" patients makes hospitals poorly suited for the care of terminal patients, whose differing needs lose out to the demands of the institutional routine. The focus on continued treatment, even in the face of inevitable death, disregards the comfort of the dying person, whose final days may be made miserable by medications or procedures that are obviously futile. Doctors and nurses, furthermore, may be unable to deal emotionally with a patient's protracted death, and the result may be that the moribund patient becomes the target of fears and aversions. Studies have actually shown, in fact, that hospital staff take significantly longer to respond to calls from moribund patients.[6]

Consequently, restructuring the physical circumstances of death has become a priority for certain parts of the thanatology movement. This restructuring generally falls into one of two patterns of alternative care. In the first, hospices are created, either independently or as special units of an existing medical facility. In a hospice, the emphasis is on the comfort, serenity, and happiness of the dying person. Life is not artificially prolonged; the orientation of the staff is affective, rather than instrumental; and hospital routines and rules are avoided. The patients bring some of their personal belongings and are encouraged to care for themselves as much as is practical. Much of the inspiration for the hospice movement in this country comes from Dr. Cicely Saunders, founder of St. Christopher's Hospice in London. The attempts to import the concept to North America have met with only modest success, and some see the long-term acceptance of hospice care jeopardized by the medical profession itself, which may perceive the movement as a threat to its prerogatives.

An alternative means of improving the quality of the final days of the dying involves arrangements that make it possible for them to remain in their own homes, receiving comfort and care in familiar surroundings. The practical requirements are considerably more difficult to assure than in a hospice, since they include insurance that pays for home care, the availability of medical and other support, of palliative care, and so forth.

A third practical endeavor of thanatologists has been to change existing laws so that individuals have the right to make certain decisions about the care they would receive if they became terminally ill. Particularly relevant is legislation that grants to the individual the right to refuse efforts to prolong his or her life.[7]

But the thanatology movement does more than address the practical concerns surrounding death, creating new programs and organizations, hospices and legislation. It is profoundly involved as well in working out new conceptions of death and of the place of the dying among us. Hence it is a creator of ideology. This is not to suggest, of course, that there is a coordinated effort to produce an ideology or creed. As in any reform movement, its ideology is the gathering sound of a plethora of different voices, expressing points of view that are often similar but by no means identical. They are perhaps better able to agree on what they oppose than on what they advocate. At the same time, the activists who are involved in education, the hospice movement, and other practical pursuits are by no means necessarily in accord with more theoretically oriented ideologues. And, like all movements, this one has its share of radicals who do not enjoy the support of all of the movement's adherents and sympathizers.

Movements need enemies—a "movement is inconceivable apart from a vital sense that some established practice or mode of thought is *wrong* and ought to be replaced."[8] While there are no doubt many means of defining an enemy, one of the simplest, and that used by the thanatology movement, involves defining an ideal, then comparing it to a woefully deficient reality. Kübler-Ross provides a classic example:

> I remember as a child (in Switzerland) the death of a farmer. He fell from a tree and was not expected to live. He asked simply to die at home, a wish that was granted without questioning. He called his daughters into the bedroom and spoke with each one of them alone for a few minutes. He arranged his affairs quietly, though he was in great pain, and distributed his belongings and his land, none of which was to be split until his wife should follow him in death. He also asked each of his children to share in the work, duties, and tasks that he had carried on until the time of the accident. He asked his friends to visit him once more, to bid good-bye to them. Although I was a small child at the time, he did not exclude me or my siblings. We were allowed to share in the preparations of the family just as we were allowed to grieve with them until he died. When he did die, he was left at home, in his own beloved home which he had built, and among his friends and neighbors who went to take a last look at him where he lay in the midst of the flowers in the place where he had lived and loved.[9]

We have only to contrast the way death is treated in this anecdote with our culture's image of death as horrific and unmentionable, which has resulted in denial and repression, exorbitant costs for unnecessary funeral practices, inhumane treatment of the dying in hospitals, ostracism of the dying by the living, unauthentic communication with the dying, and an unrealistic, mechanical, nonorganic view of life. Kübler-Ross's idyllic recollection stands in stark contrast with the pervasive terror of death in contemporary American society.

In its more popular expressions, the thanatology movement has much in common with the humanistic counterculture and its denouncement of modern Western society as dehumanizing, unemotional, unauthentic, and technologically dominated. The counterculture has embraced instead a philosophy that privileges direct sensuous experience, subjectivity, and a respect for intuition, in particular intuitive knowledge based on a naîve "openness to nature and to other people."[10] The thanatology movement embraces three sets of beliefs that have much in common with the values of the humanistic counter-culture, notably positivity, expressivity, and, somewhat strangely, immortality.

The thanatology movement is firmly rooted in the soil of a positivity that is uniquely American. Positivity is manifest in the typically American belief in progress, personal or societal, and in the conviction that life is, in the final analysis, just, or at least potentially so, and that one can get what one deserves. Such are the assumptions behind much popular psychological and religious writing. Within the context of the thanatology movement, positivity involves three basic beliefs: 1) that the dying person has a unique opportunity for "growth" and self-improvement; 2) that the death of a loved one offers a similar opportunity for family and friends; and 3) that death itself (both the moment of death and what follows) may be blissful, serene, and intensely pleasurable, perhaps even orgasmic. Such are the assumptions behind the phrase Kübler-Ross coined to describe death: "the final stage of growth." In the same vein, Marjorie McCoy, in *To Die with Style,* says: "I have sought ... a more radically positive way to view dying. I propose we look at death not primarily as a thing to be suffered but rather as an action to be anticipated and prepared for.... Why not, with Carl Jung, speak of the *achievement* of death and view dying as the final creative task of our lives?"[11]

Fortunately, it is not necessary to be dying to reap the benefits of this approach; it is enough to know someone else who is. As it says in the advertising copy for Peter Koestenbaum's *Is There an Answer to Death?:* "A positive confrontation with death can be a personally liberating experience.... It can help us to develop our individual identity and give us the security we need to live our lives courageously." Reflecting on the death of his son, Keith Kerr writes of "the benefits, insights, and awareness that have become clear to us. Such benefits include a release from guilt feelings, a release from a compulsion to 'workaholism,' a renewed sense of self-esteem, a liberating look at the inevitable fact of one's own death, and a renewed attentiveness to the 'voices' of one's own body."[12]

Finally, the positive component of this ideology offers the possibility that death and whatever follows it will be pleasurable. This sense of promise comes from the testimony of both those who have returned after being clinically dead and those who have observed the deaths of others. Robert Kavanaugh, once a priest and now a counseling psychologist, describes "the visage of the newly deceased ... often wreathed in a gentle smile or a look of uncommon peace." According to Kavanaugh, such expressions reflect a "satisfaction limited to men of any creed who died in peace. They expired without earthly strings of any kind choking their hearts and they realized that they had bequeathed no strings to choke the hearts of those they left behind."[13] Others have suggested a more tantalizing possibility. David Gordon advocates overcoming the fear of death by viewing it as "the ultimate unification experience":

> As part of his eternal cycle and ceaseless becoming, man in death merges with himself, others, and all. . . . There is an analogy here to the search for the perfect orgasm. Since time immemorial, or for as long as the recorded history of sexuality, man has attempted to perfect, prolong, and/or multiply the orgasm for himself and his partner. . . . Death does not represent destruction, evil, meaningless oblivion, or the dark forces of man. It is the quintessence of what man has always desired most and what has been the chief motivational factor in his life, the search for, and the repetition of, the spontaneous unification experience he has encountered sporadically and at random during the course of his life and existence. It is the final, ultimate and eternal experience of unity.[14]

This is not unlike the "bursting into death" (as opposed to "shrinking from it") described by Stanislav Grof in his LSD-based psychotherapy for terminally ill cancer patients. Grof sought to help the dying overcome pain, depression, and withdrawal through some kind of orgasm of consciousness. In the process the patient was to authenticate emotional closure by reviewing or reliving his or her life.[15]

The sort of idealization apparent in the examples above reveals a powerful tendency to avoid the more difficult issues raised by the rather large number of deaths that happen not to be peaceful and timely, such as deaths from painful diseases, or such sudden and violent deaths as those that occur in street crime, foreign wars, or car crashes, none of which are rarities. The examples above are also representative of the benign tenor, and even sentimentality, of much of the literature of the thanatology movement. Robert Kastenbaum has even wondered whether the "thrill of death," as it is presented in such writings, might not provoke suicides,[16] and thanatologist John Hinton writes that there is often a spurious acceptance of death among "those who are discontented with themselves, dissatisfied with the routine of their lives and frequently exhausted by their own emotional conflicts."[17] In such cases, death has become acceptable only as an alternative to the seemingly futile struggle for fulfillment, and its peace is that of abandoned hopes.

Thanatologists whose approach to death tends toward the lyrical should also be aware of the research of Zuehlke and Watkins, who conducted six sessions of Viktor Frankel's logotherapy over a two-week period with six terminally ill patients. They found significant increases in Purpose-in-Life test scores. However, there were also significant increases in their scores on the Death Anxiety Scale. (A control group showed no significant change in either score.) The results seem to suggest that while the patients receiving therapy did indeed find their lives more meaningful as a result, they also were more inclined to acknowledge a fear of death.[18] The implication is that ideologies of thanatology based on positivity would do well to balance their romanticized approach to death by addressing the very real suffering and fear that often accompany it.

A Death of One's Own: Authentic Expression

The poet Rainer Maria Rilke sensed long ago the growing chaos surrounding the issue of death, observing that it was more and more rare to find "the desire for a death of one's own." People nowadays, he observed, "die as best they can; dying the death that belongs to the disease from which they suffer ... from one of the deaths assigned to the institution; that is regarded very favorably."[19] "Dying a death of one's own" is certainly an ideal of the thanatology movement, yet, interestingly, some thanatologies may make this more difficult, rather than less so. Kübler-Ross's interviews with terminal patients led her to define five distinct stages through which the dying pass from the time they learn of their illness—denial, anger, bargaining, depression, and acceptance.[20] This schema of the dying person's response to impending death has been criticized as being perhaps less descriptive than prescriptive. Harvard psychologist Avery Weisman, for example, considers that Kübler-Ross's five stages are at best approximations and at worst obstacles to individualization.[21] The schema ignores such issues as the dying person's personality, ethnic and cultural background, earlier life experiences, and relations with both loved ones and the health care team, not to mention the cause of the imminent death. As British psychiatrist Michael Simpson has pointed out, the states of knowing and avoiding the fact of one's dying are too complex and too individual to be generalized into a one-size-fits-all model.[22] Stanley Keleman, a representative of the humanistically oriented bioenergetics movement, writes, "Most people live their dying as they have lived their lives. People who rarely express themselves emotionally, or those whose lives are lived as misery and defeat, tend to die that way. People whose lives are lived in self-expression tend to die self-expressively."[23]

The more individual a death, the less likely it is to conform to an idealized model. While Kübler-Ross and others wax lyrical over the "joy" of sharing the experience of death with the family, critics like Edwin Schneidman rightly reject the notion that the "good" death must be an easy one or that a good death requires achieving a "state of psychoanalytic grace or any other kind of closure before death sets its seal."[24] He observes that most people die too soon or too late, leaving loose ends and unfinished fragments of their life's agenda.

For Schneidman, as for Avery Weisman, the best death is simply "one that an individual would choose for himself if the choice were possible."[25] We may not be able to choose the manner of our dying, but we can, at the very least, consider the likely circumstances and perhaps take some steps to make the process more acceptable to both ourselves and our families. This includes allowing the dying person to operate on as high and effective a level and be as self-sufficient as possible. The aim is to make the final days of life full and meaningful. The dying process is worth studying so others, too, can achieve "significant survival, so that as one nears the end, one can also achieve a purposeful death."[26] The purposeful death, as Weisman defines it, is relatively pain free and involves the minimum amount of emotional and social impoverishment. An acceptable death in Weisman's scheme also includes recognizing and resolving long-standing conflicts and being satisfied that our remaining wishes are consistent with the present circumstances and with our ideal selves. Finally, we should also be able to relinquish control to others in whom we have confidence. Thus the "purposeful death" is one that allows a measure of fulfillment, quiescence, and resolution, and *perhaps* some personal development as well. This is a far more conservative vision than the highly romanticized "final stage of growth."

A final example of the ideology of authentic expression is found in the work of Lisl M. Goodman, who argues that what we fear is not so much death as the incompleteness of our lives at the moment of death. She proposes that the best defense against death, or fear of death, lies in seeking to complete our lives through creative activity. Her interviews with artists and scientists suggest that for the constantly creative, working to capacity confers a feeling of immortality. Further, since life seems most precious when we are about to lose it, full acknowledgment of death is the key to being fully alive.[27]

Life after Life

In the late 1970s, assertions concerning the existence of an afterlife emerged as an increasingly common tenet of the thanatology movement. What had begun as occasional allusions to a possibility soon emerged in the form of outright declarations. As the *Sacramento Bee* reported in October of 1975, "Dr. Elisabeth Kübler-Ross, who has counseled thousands of terminally ill patients, is convinced that 'people don't really die.' The 49-year-old Swiss-born psychiatrist ... says she knows 'beyond the shadow of a doubt' that there is life after death. 'This is not just the spooky stories of someone who has worked with too many dying patients,' she said. 'It is a good feeling to be able to say after many years that people don't really die.'"[28]

Interest in near-death experiences and the glimpses they appear to offer of an afterlife has also been stimulated by physician Raymond Moody, the most popular author currently writing on the subject.[29] Moody collected a series of reports from and interviews with people who had been close to death—in some cases actually pronounced clinically dead—but who had nonetheless revived. Their accounts tended to include such elements as hearing themselves pronounced dead; experiencing tranquility; hearing a loud ringing or buzzing sound; moving through a dark tunnel; meeting a guide, dead relatives, or friends; meeting a being composed of light; encountering a border from beyond which there could be no return; seeing visions of great knowledge, cities of light, or a realm of bewildered spirits; being rescued from physical death by a spirit; and coming back to life profoundly changed. Moody, although aware that the anecdotal nature of his material was bound to draw criticism, did not bother to provide statistics of any kind or even complete case histories. His publisher's claims to the contrary notwithstanding, Moody at least stopped short of interpreting this material as final proof of life after death.

Medical journals, too, in the 1970s, began to publish reports of patients who had had visions of an afterlife during near-death experiences, and a major journal of psychiatry, *The Journal of Nervous and Mental Disease*, set a precedent by publishing a review of the literature generated by research on reincarnation and life after death.[30] By the end of the decade, reports concerning near-death experiences had appeared in most major medical journals. A group of researchers formed the Association for the Scientific Study of Near-Death Phenomena in 1978, now the International Association for Near-Death Studies (they publish a newsletter, *Vital Signs*, as well as a quarterly journal, *Anabiosis*). Some of the more responsible articles published on the

subject in the 1970s appeared in *Omega*, an international journal publishing articles on death and related issues. Its editor, Robert Kastenbaum, noted that while near-death experiences certainly pose interest-
ing questions to researchers, near death is not the same thing as death:
"From the logical and methodological standpoint, the difference between those who stay dead and those who return may defy all efforts
to examine."[31]

Our culture's terror of death, which has resulted in a refusal to confront
or acknowledge it, has had tragic effects on how we live our lives, how
we treat our dying, even how we make nuclear policy. The thanatology
movement is a small-scale but heroic effort to alleviate this debilitating
fear. Examining the underlying ideologies of the various strands of the
movement, however, can at times be disquieting. The movement toward authentic expression reveals a keen desire to experience death
in a unique individualized way. This is consistent with the contemporary preoccupation with individualism, secularity, and materialism,
obsessions strongly implicated in the creation of death-denial in the
first place. The enthusiasm parts of the movement have shown for such
topics as near-death experiences and immortality ironically reflects a
deeply entrenched death-denial among the very people who would
eradicate it. Finally, the relentlessly positive interpretations the movement offers of death can rarely accommodate deaths that are agonizing,
violent, senseless, or otherwise fail to fit an idealized scenario. This
bias in itself reflects a reluctance to face the grimmer aspects of death.
In the final analysis, the thanatology movement, for all the good it has
done, continues in some respects to reinforce the underlying causes of
the problem it seeks to resolve.

3

Psychologies of
Consciousness and Death

Psychological theories may be thought of as maps of human consciousness, upon which are drawn the structures and processes by which the
external world is represented with the individual conscious. These
maps chart the cognitive process (the contours and boundaries of the
individual's awareness of and attention to the self, others, and the
world in which he or she exists), and they also chart territories beyond
the realm of cognitive thought processes. Each of these maps, from
which psychological interpretations and thanatologies are plotted, represents differently the region of death.

Psychology and the Nature of Consciousness

Psychology began as the study of consciousness, developing as a syn-
thesis of natural philosophy and nineteenth-century science. Emerging
as it did, simultaneously with the study of physics, psychology
adopted some of its methods and principles. In fact, in the course of its
history modern psychology has more than once been conceived of as a
kind of "physics of the soul," both in the way it states its problems and
in the nature of the theories constructed to resolve them.

In the United States, research on consciousness in the nineteenth
century was spearheaded by a group at Cornell University under E. B.
Titchener. This group sought its evidence through "introspection." In
this procedure, the observer would attempt to analyze the contents of
his own consciousness, then compare his findings with those of others
engaged in the same activity. They tended not to find much in common, and in an attempt to remedy the situation they devised some
rather strict rules. For example, an observer could not report seeing "a
book" during introspection, only an object of a certain size, shape, and

color. These and other limitations led to a certain sterility in the field, and the range of permissible inquiry became narrow. Controversies over such issues as whether or not "thoughts without images" could occur dominated the discipline, and psychologists' attention drifted further and further from their original concerns. Since the cognitive maps of any two individuals were never the same, this approach proved a dead end.

John Watson opened the gates once again with his suggestion that psychology study action, which was, after all, observable and testable. Behaviorism was "objective" and "scientific" and it permitted the study of major problems left out of the introspective paradigm. Soon behaviorism dominated American psychology. As with introspection, however, the scope of inquiry within psychology became limited to problems amenable to solution by its own methods. Psychologists began to ignore or even deny the existence of phenomena that did not fit the behaviorist schema, such as consciousness, which for many years was not even a subject of research. When behaviorism as a useful tool became confused with behaviorism as the total extent of knowledge, consciousness and the functioning of the brain were equated.[1] The rational mind was considered merely a property of neurological functioning, and physiological processes were the causal explanation for all experiential phenomena. In this view, the mind, consciousness, and the brain are identical. Objective facts were valued to the exclusion of any question not subject to a logical, verbal answer, rather in the manner of the logical positivists, who maintained that any question not amenable to a perfectly logical answer should not be asked.

Some psychologists, of course, continued to entertain questions about the nature of consciousness, but even they did so in terms derived from the natural sciences. "The mechanics of the soul," as developed by Hebart, explains psychic life mechanically in terms of ideas attracting and repelling each other reciprocally, the first idea actually attracting the next idea to emerge from the unconscious, in which it preexisted. Hebartian psychology, dominant for several decades in Austria and Germany, was sharply attacked toward the end of the nineteenth century, yet elements of it have managed to survive in several forms. One example lies in the psychoanalytic theory of the repression of desires and of other emotional tendencies whose gratification is forbidden by collective morality. The "psychic censor"—the representative and executor of morality—does not tolerate that such desires should even present themselves to consciousness. Consequently, they retreat into the unconscious, emerging occasionally to manifest themselves as dreams, as slips of the tongue, and, after diverse transformations, as neurotic symptoms.

Freud interpreted both normal and pathological psychical phenomena in terms of his unified conception of libido as a form of energy. For Freud, the human psyche resembled a closed physical system endowed with a certain quantity of energy. Energy can be distributed in diverse ways; it can exist in a variety of forms; it can change the mode of its manifestations; but, it can neither be diminished nor augmented. Working from this paradigm, Freud sought to discover a single driving force behind all human attitudes and activities, however diverse these manifestations might appear at first sight. He reduced them all to elementary forms of the libido, those it assumes at the beginning and in the early stages of life.

Philosophy, Science, and the Exploration of Consciousness

In psychology that has been "scientized," depending upon the scientific method of experimentation with reproducible and quantifiable results, the potential exists for a preoccupation with technology. This is an example of what philosopher William Barrett describes as the "worldless consequence of Cartesian philosophy."[2] Descartes distinguished mind and body in such a way that their activities seemed disconnected. This established a rift between the mind and external things. Consciousness was conceived of as essentially outside of the world in which it exists, but with power over it. Descartes gave philosophical formulation to the procedures on which science was already embarked, and he proposed that these procedures be extended to all domains of human inquiry.

In Descartes's subject-object distinction, the two terms are not equal; the first term, the subject, asserts its priority. The quest for certainty led Descartes to affirm the existence of the conscious ego (ego cogitans) as the central certainty. The conscious ego, as subject, extends this initial certainty over the object, which it impoverishes of all qualities except those relevant to its own purposes. The subject separates itself from the object in order to ensure its own mastery over it. Dualism is human self-assertion in the face of nature.

Here, in outline, is the metaphysics that lies behind the technological era. It has exacted a heavy toll in that it has disparaged the human bond with the physical world. The mind now confronts a nature that, because of the mind's own conceptions, has become alien to it. Nature has become a realm of objects whose objectivity consists precisely in those quantifiable aspects that permit calculation and control. Nature has come to be thought of as mere material for exploitation, with humanity towering over it as master.

It is no accident that the rise of modern science was accompanied by the articulation of a particular kind of consciousness. As conscious beings, we humans belong to the realm of subjectivity, separated from the objective world. This subjective realm is privileged in a most important respect. Consciousness is the general medium of constitution. The universe of objects and the world of everyday experience, as well as the scientific representation of the world, exist for human beings only through acts of consciousness. Claims for objectivity and validity depend on the constituting power of consciousness. As a study of consciousness, psychology can be assigned a place within the system of the sciences. It is not one science among the others; instead, it is their foundation. Its main task is not to enrich our knowledge of reality, as the physical and chemical sciences do, but to account for the very knowledge of reality.

Recently, schools of thought have emerged that attempt to transcend objectivist bias by taking the subjective realities of the person into account. Psychologists like Charles Tart, for example, espouse emergent interactionism; that is, brain and mind as dualistic aspects combined to form a system. Consciousness is a property of this system (not just of brain alone) and manifests itself as "states," of which rational, conceptual thought is only one.[3]

The existential-phenomenological psychologists and many philosophers regard consciousness as intentional; that is, consciousness is always consciousness *of*—it always has an object that is not consciousness itself.[4] Consciousness is the process by which meaning is revealed, and human experience and meaning constitute the primary reality.

In the religious and spiritual realms, consciousness is identified with a transpersonal, nondualistic reality. Pure consciousness is the absolute, nominal ground that underlies all apparent phenomenal distinctions. Brain, mind, matter, and meaning become reflections or manifestations of an underlying, all-encompassing unity or transcendent consciousness. From this perspective, which distinguishes everyday experience from mystical union (this union being the true origin and ultimate goal), consciousness is consciousness *without* an object—pure, undifferentiated bliss. Intentionality may indeed characterize mind but is not a hallmark of consciousness. The traditional dualisms are also seen in a new light. Subject-object, mind-matter, idealism-realism, and knower-known are all considered to be illusory dichotomies, their fundamental unity being more basic than their apparent difference.

Quantum physics and neuropsychology, and such life sciences as ethology, have recently evolved holistic theoretical formulations that treat consciousness in a way remarkably similar to the mystical approaches discussed above, a promising development in the relations between the nominal and phenomenal realms.

In our consideration of the maps of consciousness proposed by those psychological theories on which the thanatology movement is founded, we must keep in mind the effects of psychological dualism. We shall note its contribution to a radical subjectivism that separates humanity from the world in which it exists and prevents it from either recalling its past or anticipating its future. Overcoming this dualism may be an essential step in making death something we can envision as part of human life.

Psychoanalytic Theory and Consciousness

Freud's hypotheses concerning the human fear of death are fundamental to the thought of psychoanalytically oriented thanatologists. In Freud's view, since "nothing resembling death can ever be experienced,"[5] we cannot truly conceive of our own mortality: "At bottom, no one believes in his own death, or, to put the same thing in another way ... in the unconscious, every one of us is convinced of his own immortality."[6] Consequently, although the fear of death "dominates us more than we know,"[7] it is not death itself that we actually fear. The fear of death, he believed, is a secondary fear that receives cognitive content from other sources, and is "usually the outcome of a sense of guilt."[8] The result of such thinking has been that much subsequent Freudian theory about death has turned away from death itself as a source of anxiety, looking instead for the psychosexual conflicts—for example, castration anxiety—that it assumes to lie beneath.[9]

While Freud more or less dismissed the conceptual centrality of death, he was nonetheless profoundly aware of his own fear of death, and he wrote with great insight on the psychological costs of denying death. Moreover, he provided the beginning of a unitary view of life and death in the one area in which he accorded death conceptual importance—the "death instinct." The death instinct was the the ultimate source of all self-destructiveness, which included aggression and violence (seen as self-destructiveness turned outward). In opposition to the death instinct was the sexual energy and love generated by the "life instincts."

One result of this view, however, is a reductionist entrapment within which it becomes all but impossible to explore important questions—for instance, those of psychic representations (imaging) and psychic energy. Thus psychoanalysts who have followed Freud have tended to jettison the death instinct altogether, losing in the process the unitary vision of which it was a part and increasingly discounting the idea of death as important to human motivation. Psychoanalytically oriented depth psychology tends to ignore questions of death imaging.

Freud believed that primitive man had two opposing unconscious attitudes toward death, simultaneously acknowledging it as the annihilation of life and denying it as unreal. He held that we have embraced only the denial—at severe psychological cost. Writing against the general fascination with death he saw operating in World War I, he made an eloquent plea for greater psychological honesty: "Would it not be better to give death a place in reality and in our thoughts which is its due, and to give a little more prominence to the unconscious attitude toward death which we have hitherto so carefully suppressed? ... If you want to endure life, prepare yourself for death."[10]

Psychiatrist Gregory Zilboorg follows Freud in believing that under ordinary circumstances human beings do not believe in their own mortality. We go about our business, "marshalling all forces which still the voice reminding us that our end must come someday."[11] However, this defense mechanism tends to break down when we are confronted with imminent catastrophe. The dying may suffer from a variety of psychological torments. A person with a weak ego, finding himself in the final stages of life, may regard his life as having been useless and wasted and may spend his last days agonizing over lost opportunities. Another, who seems to yearn for death, may be suffering either consciously or unconsciously from guilt, and regard death as just punishment. Psychoanalysts believe that those who have spent their lives as aggressive, dominant people are much more inclined to experience intense fear in the face of death, unable to accept the loss of control over their destinies. Conversely, the humble and submissive tend to be better prepared to abandon life. People tend to interpret death through the lens of their preoccupations in life. For example, a dying man who has been preoccupied throughout his life with a fear of losing his potency may identify with death as a castrator.

According to Kurt Eissler, patients with life-threatening illnesses are instinctively aware of the imminence of death, even if they cannot articulate that awareness, and it is the therapist's task to help them confront this knowledge and accept it.[12] The therapist may be better able than the friends and family of the dying to deal rationally with the dying person's fears and, through a combination of warmth and detachment, can bring tangible relief. The therapist, rather than urging the patient to forget his fears, encourages him to remember—to bring hidden fears into the open and work to resolve them. This is the first step in therapy and in many cases the only one needed. The second step, if necessary, involves trying to translate symptoms back to their original form, on the assumption that every symptom is a signal or symbol of an unconscious fear. In exploring these symptoms, we find our instinctual fears, and by identifying these we can grow, expand our horizons, and find a path to an accurate and acceptable self-image. Psychotherapy, by addressing the sources of such symptoms as guilt, denial, anxiety, depression, narcissism, and apathy, permits the insights that can release us from them. Another strategy for dealing with the fears of the dying, who frequently wait passively for the end, involves arousing their creative impulses, stimulating renewed interest as either a producer or consumer of art.

These are some of the methods psychoanalytically oriented therapists use to enhance the quality of life for the dying. But despite the clearly important aims of promoting self-acceptance and reconciliation with others, psychoanalytic approaches, based on the Freudian concept of consciousness, work primarily on the patient's subjectivity. Freud came upon the fear of death while exploring the intricacies of intrapsychic dynamics, and perceived it as a product of prior psychic events and experiences. Consequently, in the psychoanalytic schema there is no real encounter with the fear of death. The complex internal dynamics that result in other issues presenting themselves in the guise of a fear of death take precedence, in the psychoanalytic map of consciousness, over the reality of personal extinction.

Existential-Phenomenological Psychology and Consciousness

There is another analysis of consciousness that is both more expansive and less mechanistic. The late French phenomenologist Maurice Merleau-Ponty endeavored to show that human experience and behavior occupy an order of being intermediate between ideas and mechanisms, showing characteristics of both realms, yet fully belonging to neither.[13] The phenomenological investigation of consciousness returns to the immediacy of lived experience, eschewing explanations and suspending all questions of causes to remain within an internal, descriptive, structural analysis. Phenomenology, however, is by no means a mere inventory of the feelings, ideas, and awareness that flow on the surface of experience (consciousness in that sense would be no more than that of which one is focally aware at a given moment). Instead, phenomenology is concerned with the organizational principles that govern the relationship of the conscious organism with the world, consequently determining the momentary contents of consciousness. The key insight of phenomenology is that human thought and activity connect person and world, subject and object, and establish a relationship in between, thus overcoming the cartesian separation of subject and object.

Phenomenological psychology is deeply concerned with questions of meaning in life. Whereas Freudian thought is expressed in dynamic, energistic terms that convey images of doing, this map of consciousness is much more concerned with being. Central to this analysis is nonbeing; that is, death. "The essential, basic arch-anxiety (primal anxiety) is innate to all isolated, individual forms of human existence. In the basic anxiety human experience is afraid of as well as anxious about its 'being-in-the-world.'"[14]

The existential emphasis in phenomenology comes from the acceptance of the importance of the body and the realization that human subjectivity is an embodied and corporeal subjectivity—what Merleau-Ponty called the "body-subject."[15] This expansion of meaning to include the preconscious and precognitive dimensions of human existence opened up the whole realm of prereflective body-world relationships, which affect us, often without our being aware of it.

The existential-phenomenological school of thought has given rise to both humanistic and gestalt psychologies. Not surprisingly, given its emphasis on meaning and being, much of the thanatology movement is grounded in existential-phenomenological thought, and much popular literature on thanatological issues reflects its concept of consciousness. In a general way, phenomenological-existential psychology can be represented by the thought of Ernest Becker, Stanley Keleman, and Peter Koestenbaum.

In spite of the twentieth century's aversion to the thought of death, the body remains as an inescapable reminder of mortality. Ernest Becker's work is, in part, a statement on the nature of human embodiment and the fear of death that accompanies it. The body, as Becker puts it, is a universal problem to the creature that must die.[16] His central thesis is that nothing haunts humanity like the fear of death, and that this fear is in fact the mainspring of human activity, which seeks to overcome death through denial. Becker states that what people really want is heroism: "The problem of heroics is the central one of human life ... the universal human problem." The drive to be heroic is, in Becker's terms, simply the drive toward "what might be called 'cosmic significance.'"[17] The combination of natural narcissism with the basic need for self-esteem results in a creature that needs to feel itself an object of primary value, first in the universe, representing in itself all of life. Heroism, in Becker's description, simply means the desire to be in control of the cosmos, godlike.

At the same time, heroism avoids anything that subtracts from its cosmocentricity. Death is the ultimate subtraction and consequently the ultimate terror; "the repression of death is the primary repression."[18] Within this context, Becker is simultaneously sympathetic with and critical of Freud's concept of the death instinct, a "device that enabled [Freud] to keep intact earlier instinct theory by attributing human evil to a deeper organic substratum than merely ego conflict with sexuality."[19] This instinctual model, he points out, "allowed Freud to keep the terror of death outside his formulation [and avoid seeing that terror] as a primary human problem of ego mastery."[20]

Becker, however, falls into his own reductionism by building a psychology that attempts to overcome the fear of death. He follows Otto Rank in substituting consciousness of death for Freud's sexuality as the ultimate motivator within the human psyche: "*This* is what is creaturely about man, *this* is the repression on which culture is built."[21] Terrified by awareness of death, we can only fall back on comforting illusions, like belief in immortality and the cohesiveness of the personality beyond death. In retaining the compensatory ethos that has so long plagued depth psychology, Becker cannot avoid creating a series of dualisms of his own: the "truth" of death versus the "lie" of character, culture, and immortality; the doomed body versus the eternal reach of the mind; the rational fact of death versus the quest for immortality.

Furthermore, the absence in Becker's work of a sense of the full significance of symbolization, particularly the symbolization of the life process, has been remarked upon by Robert Jay Lifton.[22] Without it, Becker's thanatology can offer little in the way of a theory of vitality or life, and his work lacks a fully realized unitary life/death paradigm. In addition, Lucy Bregman has pointed out in Becker's work a representation of a self entirely removed from all that the earth represents, a self in one sense grandiose but at the same time profoundly depleted in many ways.[23] Becker's paradigm neglects cultural and contextual factors in favor of explanations forged in terms of universal human nature. Becker's vision of the self may represent a rather traditional response to a lack of meaning, heroism, and trust in both the individual psyche and society.

Regardless of these criticisms, Becker provides a theoretical context for widening the investigation of consciousness from intrapsychic concerns to more inclusive concepts. For example, he interprets psychoanalysis's concept of the anal stage as descriptive of the period in a child's life when it begins to turn its attention to its own body, and when the mind begins to differentiate itself from the body, so that the body becomes object to the mind.[24] The urge to heroism—the attempt to be cosmocentric and immortal—results in focus shifting to the recalcitrant body, the locus of life and death. Becker's reinterpretation of the anal stage is very different from the psychoanalytic origin of the concept, which involved a reduction to sexual drives and early conflicts. Rather than interpreting the fear of death as a manifestation of intrapsychic conflict, Becker sees intrapsychic conflict as a means of coping with the fear of death. Becker's vision encompasses knowing what it means to die, as well as knowing that one is destined to die.

Stanley Keleman's thought has added important contours to the existential-phenomenological map of consciousness. An advocate of the psychotherapeutic system called bioenergetics, he approaches the cartesian subject-object split by emphasizing the event that occurs when the one encounters the other. Keleman's work addresses not only the subject-object split but also the mind-body split. In his view, if consciousness exists almost exclusively in the head, then one simply becomes a head that owns a body. For many people, the body is an object of projection that is not-self. The ego, as a rule, becomes identified exclusively with voluntary processes, while the body becomes an object "out there." The result is the separation and isolation of the psychic from the somatic, and of surface phenomena from their roots in the depths of the organism. Thus, loss of awareness of one's own body is only the most apparent sign of a disruption of the entire organism. Reintegrating mind and body is one of the primary focuses of Keleman's therapeutic approach.[25]

When the projected body is alienated, Keleman believes, it returns to haunt one with a variety of somatic complaints that are, in reality, manifestations of one's own energy. While not all practitioners in the burgeoning field of psychosomatic medicine would agree with the nuances of Keleman's theories, they are certainly unanimous in asserting the importance of the relationship between psyche and soma in disease processes.

When the ego, recoiling from the body's susceptibility to pain and suffering, seeks to withdraw awareness from the body, it simultaneously numbs the flesh and distorts consciousness. Obviously the ego cannot control the body's involuntary sensations, but it can and does desensitize it. Keleman is among those psychotherapists who seek to remind us that in numbing the source of pain, we also numb the source of pleasure. His aim is to enable people to establish a sense of identity with the entire psychophysical organism, discovering an authentic, existential self. This involves focusing intensely on the tension existing at various points within our bodies and concentrating on releasing it. In doing so, we become aware of the artificiality inherent in the concepts of the voluntary and the involuntary, the willed and the spontaneous. To the extent that we manage to feel these processes as processes of the self, we can begin to to accept as perfectly natural all manner of things we cannot control. More at ease with the spontaneous and more accepting of the uncontrollable, we develop a faith in a deeper self than the mere ego and learn to accept this self even though we may not always be in control of it. When our concept of ourselves embraces the involuntary as well as the voluntary, we no longer perceive ourselves as victims, either of our bodies or of such spontaneous and uncontrollable processes as death.

Keleman sees death as a natural continuation, rather than an interruption, of life, and one, in fact, that makes growth possible.[26] In calling for "dying one's own death,"[27] Keleman is urging that we read our own interior messages, focusing upon the organism in order to establish greater conscious control over the process of dying.

Keleman's conception of death as process is the logical systemic extension of his concept of life as process. The self that participates in life is made up of a governing "board of directors, without a permanent chairman."[28] This board of directors is made up of all the identifiable characters that make up the self: feelings and sensations, images, memory, biological mechanisms, sexuality, and one's sense of universality. It is the interaction of these elements that creates each person's personal mythology. For the dying, living their own myth means realizing that "they are their own death."[29] Keleman declares that each person is more than consciousness, or body, or social roles, all of which must end with death. The dying, if they are to discover life, and hence death, as process, must abandon their preoccupation with memory, which binds them to the past, and with projection, which binds them to the future, in favor of awareness of the experience of life in the present. Only in this way can the dying free themselves from society's mythology of death and cultivate their own experience. "Persons who embrace the culture's values and succeed in their lives on its terms may be said to be living the culture's life. They may also be said to be living its death...."[30] To decide to live our own dying is to accept responsibility for both our living and our dying and to decide to fully live them both. The result, as Keleman sees it, is that we are freed from seeing ourselves as victimized by death. The decision to die frees us from a mechanistic, routine death, which reflects the mythology of the culture at large, in favor of a personal death, which reflects our own. "The person who loves life, who participates in their dying, can risk living creatively and dying so."[31]

Peter Koestenbaum's work is a reaction against the contemporary cultural theory he calls the "ghost-in-a-machine" approach to human consciousness, a theory that is mechanistic, technological, and materialistic, and which promotes attempts to cure death rather than attempts to understand it as a part of life. He calls his discipline "personalized education in philosophy."[32] Typical of many phenomenological-existential thinkers, he assumes that many of the most important issues in psychotherapy are philosophical rather than psychological or medical, and his concern is to show how the marriage of philosophy and health is the logical culmination of the history of philosophy. Koestenbaum's orientation necessarily leads him into questions of meaning and self-actualization, and he is concerned with both the negative (empty) aspects of existence—anxiety, suffering, guilt—and the positive (substantial) ones—love and the phenomena of encounter with the world and with others and intersubjectivity.

   Death, for Koestenbaum, "explains what it is to be human (searching for meaning, immortality, freedom, love, and individuality) far better than the psychological principles of sex and aggression, the biological instincts of survival and procreation, the utilitarian theories of happiness and approbation, or the religious ukase of God's will."[33] Death reveals both the individual and the cosmic self, for people are both temporal and eternal, empirical and transcendental. First of all, death reveals us as individual and particular. Death need not appear tragic because confronting death, accepting it, and integrating it fully into our experience makes life itself rich and full. "To be human," as Koestenbaum says, "means to freely choose one's finitude."[34]

   Consciousness of death can bring awareness of our finitude, of the individual aspects of being human, which in turn can neutralize fear and energize life. It can lead to decisiveness by allowing us to perceive what is essential and what is not, and as we find meaning in life, we can become more honest, strong, and assertive, breaking the stranglehold of failure and laying plans for how to live our lives. At the same time, death can make each person conscious of a silent and solitary center, the eternal within us; it can make us aware of ourselves as spiritual and transpersonal beings. The consequences of the discovery of this eternal dimension can include a sense of peace and freedom, accompanied by a burst of creative energy. Finally comes the integration of the twin awarenesses of both our finitude and our immortality. "Only through the reminder of death do I understand that I am more than a body, more than a personality, more than a name—I am also a consciousness, one that is aware of my body, of my personality, of my name, but is not to be confused with them."[35] In keeping with phenomenological-existential precepts, consciousness of death is not merely a concept but actually an accessible region of being, one that can be reached only by confronting the death of the self.

Not surprisingly, anyone absorbed in the world of objects will be overwhelmed with anxiety to discover that he or she is also consciousness: Anxiety is the "result of the immediate disclosure of consciousness in itself,"[36] rather than an unconscious conflict, a psychopathology, or material from the unconscious threatening the defenses of the ego. In existential thought, upon which the growth movement Koestenbaum represents is based, the fundamental cognitive condition is anxiety, and existential psychologists use death anxiety to explore the foundations of human existence. They understand anxiety as rooted in the discovery and experience of groundlessness, an eternal fall in infinite space without permanent existence. The acting out of this experience is the fear of death. Death is merely a symbol for this pervasive underlying anxiety—an anxiety that reveals the condition of human existence.

Koestenbaum's psychotherapy, then, postulates two responses to death: first, the creation of the self as a living and committed individual; and second, the establishment of a pure, detached awareness that one is part of something beyond death. Although we are individuals only to the extent that we are separated from the spatiotemporal infinity that envelops us, comfort lies in identifying ourselves with all of nature or with the cosmic stream of consciousness. Of course, anyone who fails to balance the temporal and the eternal, who recognizes only the cosmic, will believe that he or she is a consciousness that will never die. The fear of death is vanquished, but only at the price of abandoning the unique individuality that we call the person.

The existentialist resolves this dilemma by recognizing that we are simultaneously isolated, finite individuals *and* part of the the cosmic space-time consciousness. The sense of unity with being can occur regardless of whether we identify with and focus on the subjective realm (ourselves as part of the cosmic consciousness) or the objective realm (ourselves as part of the stream of life, nature, and evolution).

Both are authentic alternatives in which death has a natural place and need not be feared.

Koestenbaum sees the experience of deathlessness, which is also the experience of egolessness, as life's highest value; no sacrifice is too great to make in order to truly experience this insight. For Koestenbaum, death permits us to understand and appreciate the eternity of consciousness: "We have challenged ... nature by inventing death, so that we can, in the act of philosophically overcoming death, be reminded of the eternity of our consciousness."[37]

The phenomenological-existential concept of consciousness exemplified in Koestenbaum's work addresses issues of self-actualization, questions of meaning, and life-death concerns, proposing as a solution the cultivation of a whole-bodied, full-minded awareness that floods the mind and body and includes the entire psychophysiological being. To identify with both the ego and the body is actually to alter both by setting each in a new context. The consciousness that results is not a fact or state of affairs, but rather a relation, a matrix for events, a precondition for meaningful being. Consciousness is no longer restricted to subjectivity, as it was by Descartes and the modern tradition of philosophy, but arises through the interaction of subject and object. The ego can reach down to earth—its ground and support—and the body can reach up to heaven—its light and space. The boundary between them has been dissolved and the struggle resolved, producing a deeper unity. The inevitability of death becomes the most vitalizing fact of life. The present moment, once perceived in relation to our eventual death, becomes meaningful, and the thought of death suffuses life with a liberating sense of urgency, an increased awareness in the way we conduct our lives.

Consciousness in Analytical Psychology

Carl Jung, like Freud, believed in the dichotomy of the conscious and the unconscious, but Jung's vision of the unconscious was radically different. He had found that primitive images familiar to him from his studies of the world's many mythologies appeared regularly and unmistakably in the dreams and fantasies of modern Europeans, the great majority of whom were entirely unfamiliar with the myths in question. Jung reasoned that since these people had not encountered these mythological images during their lifetimes, these basic motifs must be structures inherent in humanity. The primordial images, or archetypes, as Jung called them, consequently were collective and transcendent.[38] While parts of the unconscious contain personal memories, wishes, and ideas, the deeper, collective realm of the unconscious contains nothing whatsoever that is unique to the individual. Instead, it houses the motifs common to the entire human race—the gods, goddesses, demons, heroes, and villains that have found expression in the world's ancient mythologies. All live on, in condensed form, in the depths of the unconscious and can profoundly affect us in both creative and destructive ways. It is the aim of transpersonal therapies like Jung's to help us consciously acknowledge and harness these forces, rather than allowing them to drive us without our knowledge and contrary to our desires. This therapy has been called "learning to live life mythologically,"[39] and requires that we grasp the transcendent and see it alive in ourselves, in others, and in our environment. This is not to say that we must abandon the conventional world and retreat into mythic fantasies, but simply that we can revitalize our daily existence by reconnecting it to a much deeper source.

According to Jung, a particular situation in someone's life will activate a particular, corresponding archetype, which then exerts an influence on the person's behavior that may range from mild to extreme. The archetype may also begin to manifest itself in dreams, fantasies, or hallucinations, perhaps as a sphinx, gorgon, serpent, winged horse, or other archetypal creature. Understanding the archetype's role in ancient mythologies, what the image has meant to other human beings, can lead to an understanding of how it functions in the unconscious of the contemporary individual. Awareness of the archetype's transpersonal meaning allows one greater understanding and permits access to one's inner depths. The growth that results is simultaneously growth of the self and a transcendence of the self.

The more universal perspective achieved by the expansion of consciousness to the transcendent or transpersonal plane means that we are no longer as preoccupied with our own personal vantage point. We are more able to examine our individual concerns with creative detachment, realizing that the deeper self can transcend problems we may face as individuals, remaining untouched, free, and open.

Analytical psychology's approach to the transcendent self has been applied to the issue of death anxiety in the work of Edgar Herzog. Herzog has observed that anyone who has been in close contact with death, either through personal risk, as in war, or through the death of a loved one, knows "with special poignancy that the ability to endure the presence of death in life is of decisive importance for human living."[40] He also notes, however, the denial of death that pervades our culture, the result, perhaps, of an "excess" of death that has produced a tendency to refuse to think about death altogether. Thus the psyche fails to come to grips with "the basic conditions of human life." The outcome has been the inhibition of real becoming and its replacement by an external air of security that is, in fact, continually threatened by unconscious anxieties that give rise to neuroses.[41]

A good example of Herzog's method can be seen in his analysis of a myth from Ceram in the Molucca Islands: In the primordial past, Hainuwele, a divine maiden, appeared from a tree and began to shower rich gifts upon the people. Their initial delight palled, however, when the flow of gifts, which showed no signs of ending, seemed to threaten the balance and harmony of their lives. They resolved to do away with her, and one night as they danced about her, they threw her into a pit. The next day her father found the body, dismembered it, and buried the pieces separately. Each was transformed into something previously unknown, including what henceforth became the staple food of the people. Hainuwele's father gave her arms to another divine maiden, Mulua Satene, the ruler of mankind. Infuriated by the crime, she built a gate, telling the people that only those who passed through the gate would remain human. Those who passed though the gate she touched with the arms of Hainuwele, and those who did not were transformed into animals and spirits. Since that time human beings have had to die and take a difficult journey to find Mulua Satene again.[42]

Herzog proposes that this myth contains a fourfold interpretation of the relationship between life and death. First, humanity is unable to endure life's unending abundance, which, by leading to murder, brings death into the world. Second, that which dies is transformed into food and food is transformed into life. Thus, life itself means transformation. Third, as the divine Mulua Satene makes clear, only those who are prepared to pass through the gates of death, to be touched by death, can remain human. The encounter with death must be made consciously, and this is what distinguishes humanity from the animal world. Fourth, the encounter with death brings with it awareness of another aspect of existence, since consciousness of death reflects back upon and illuminates the other frontier of life, birth.

The experience of encountering death, according to Herzog, may be thought of as an opportunity for the "religious growth of the soul."[43] The myth of Ceram is taken to mean that only those who are psychically ready to pass through the gate of death can continue to be human. What is required is not merely the acceptance of the fact of death but also the inclusion of death in life. When death is included in life, the myth implies, we leave behind our limited existence in the present and are confronted with a transformation that, however frightening, is fruitful. The awareness that we exist in the past and the future, as well as in the present, is specifically human.

Herzog's psychotherapeutic practice assumes that inner crises of transformation are often foreshadowed by dreams of a confrontation of death, either directly or in the form of an archaic image. The panic created by the image of death can be overcome by realizing that it can become an image of transformation. The neurotic, in Herzog's schema, is sick because he or she cannot accept transformation, clinging instead to fantasies of changelessness, though these may be destructive and manifestly false. (The neurotic has a friend in modern science, for its apparent omnipotence suggests that death is an event that need not really occur after all.) When these fantasies begin to break down in the course of therapy, the patient's first response is to feel delivered over to death, which is why dreams of encounters with death are often indicators of the beginnings of transformation. When life's realities force transformation, the person also encounters the reality of death and must come to terms with both. The struggle to elucidate and accept the death-image is an essential one for many patients, whether or not they are aware of it. When we understand the nature of dreams of death and set them within the context of this therapy as a whole, we can see that the dreams are associated with growing courage and an increasing readiness to face crises of personality transformation. Herzog terms the stages of growth such dreams indicate as "fundamentally religious." What is involved is a growing acceptance of death as a condition of life, an acceptance accompanied by a transformation of the whole person.

Herzog's highly imaginative explorations of the psychology of death, emerging from the Jungian tradition and drawing upon mythic and religious themes, are something of an anomaly in contemporary psychological discourse. His insistence that symbols and myths are the true stuff of the psyche and his rejection of approaches that reduce such images to mere mystifications designed to protect the symbolizer from reality represent a movement away from ego-dominated psychology. It also contrasts sharply with our culture's emphasis on physical, rather than psychic, life; on the literal and material, rather than the metaphorical and spiritual. From the perspective of Herzog's map of consciousness, denial of death is hardly a normal reaction, attributable to universal human nature. Instead, death denial is a symptom of the dominion of the ego and of the loss of wholeness this entails. A defensive attitude toward death represents the external, literal, and material assertion of the ego as it seeks to adapt "to outer reality." The recognition of death, on the other hand, suggests "self-subordination to inner reality."[44] The transformation Herzog describes is a matter of becoming aware of existence as part of a meaningful order that both includes and transcends the individual. We first respond to death as something that is "totally other," the antithesis and negation of what we know as life. But we come to see that this "other" actually belongs, of necessity, to life and to realize that death impinges upon existence at the point at which existence extends beyond life.

In Herzog's conception, existence in the present is thought to take place in a world that is largely hidden yet gives meaning and order to the present. Within this hidden matrix, neither life nor death is an independent power. Rather, both are manifestations of the archetype of divinity, which includes both life and death within itself and rules over them. Death becomes a spiritual event, only one of the instruments, though an important one, of the archetype of divinity.

Conclusion

In much contemporary psychology, the response to death is built upon the Stoic assumption that death belongs to the natural order of things as much as birth does, and we must live and act according to nature. The syllogistic reasoning behind this form of ethical naturalism is that each of us is a natural being, that death is a natural event, and that we must therefore learn to accept it. Consequently, in much psychoanalytically or psychodynamically oriented literature there are few explicit references to any ultimate or cosmic dimension of existence. One of the largely unquestioned assumptions of contemporary secular society is that birth, sex, and death are simply successive stages in what is essentially a mechanical process. Gail Sheehy's bestseller, *Passages*,[45] implicitly endorses this world-view, in which life is a horizontal progression toward greater autonomy and is devoid of any religious or transcendent dimension. At the end of this process, death arrives to spur any last minute "passages" before time runs out. Unassociated with any true symbolic meaning, Sheehy's "passages" reflect a purely mechanistic vision of existence. Indeed, for the most part, psychology, in its search for scientific respectability, has tended to construct mechanistic models that simply feed North America's preoccupation with technology, and psychology has to some extent become the technology of explaining and controlling the human mind.

Some of the psychotherapies reviewed in this chapter, however, are founded on theories that suppose another dimension to human existence. Even Becker, with his emphasis on human beings as creatures, employs the image of the ascension of the self to the point at which it can escape the limited logic of the earth and confront the mystery and wonder of the cosmos. Koestenbaum's theory relies upon a multileveled view of human experience and draws upon the ancient concept of cosmic layers, while Herzog's psychomythology assumes a split between daily experience and the archetype. With the movement toward a more vertical comprehension of the nature of human experience comes a need for a radical change in the metaphysical and cosmological ideas that have resulted from the dominance of Western scientific thought. The time has arrived, as Robert Ornstein has written, for "dealing with a psychology which can speak of a 'transcendence of time as we know it ... ' [and for] extending the boundaries of inquiry of modern science, extending our concept of what is possible for man."[46] A complete catalog of current attempts in this direction among psychiatrists and psychologists would reveal the influences of Zen and Tibetan Buddhism, Sufism, Hinduism in its various forms, and, lately, even the practices of early monastic and Eastern Christianity, as well as such remnants of the mystical Judaic tradition as Cabala and Hasidism.

A growing concern with the metaphysics of awareness or of consciousness appears even among the hard sciences. Neurobiologist John Eccles has sought to revive in people "a belief in their spiritual nature superimposed on their material body and brain,"[47] and is exploring the possibility of self-recognition and communication after death in ways we are presently unable to imagine. Ethologist John H. Crook has decried the dichotomy existing between biology and a metaphysics of awareness, observing that ethologists have devoted themselves so exclusively to the study of behavior that, like behavioral psychologists, they have omitted to study the origins of the human mind. In his view, ancient theories from cultures other than our own represent more profound analysis than we have yet managed, and Buddhism in particular, by virtue of a "subjective empiricism" has systematically explored the question of states of consciousness to a degree not yet attained in modern Western societies.[48] Indeed, in contrast to many of the thanatologists whose work we have examined, Crook is willing seriously to engage questions of meaning and mortality in relation to death: "Death-awareness and self-awareness are essentially two sides of the same coin, for the discovery that the body dies implies the ending also of personal experience. The problem that has teased man has centered around the question of whether this is really so. The dread of death is the dread of the termination of personal experience. It is cleverly anchored in the attachment to the construct of self as an identity."[49]

Yet the search for a satisfactory psychological approach to death will require a more comprehensive map of consciousness, one which must first of all move beyond both biological and reductionist orientations. It must be flexible enough to take into account the fears, hopes, and dreams of the individual and to allow for the fact that death may have quite different meanings depending on whether the dying person is twenty or seventy. Above all, an adequate map of consciousness must acknowledge the inclusiveness of human experience; in other words, it must have a religious dimension, a several-storied world of existence that allows a fresh perspective on the significance of death. Finally, such a map of consciousness must affirm the importance of social and historical experience, an expanded horizontal dimension of the self that can allow escape from the debilitating trends of technocracy and radical individualism.

4

Transpersonal Psychologies, Sacred Tradition, and Death

The movement broadly known as transpersonal psychology has arisen in response to the failure of other psychologies to address questions of meaning in human life, one of these questions being the meaning of death. Much of its theory and method has been based on Eastern religious thought and practices, as well as upon the Judeo-Christian meditative tradition, and the desire for transformation is among its hallmarks. Jacob Needleman has described contemporary society as existing between dreams as, disillusioned with the dream of a technological utopia, we grope for another source of hope; the personal transformation proposed by transpersonal psychologies corresponds to Needleman's second dream.

The transpersonal perspective is concerned with the experience of unity, of fundamental wholeness, of the superconscious All. It rejects the existence of entities who are separate, bounded, and isolated, whether things, people, or God. The realization of the connectedness of all things entails the death of the separate and isolated self, the voluntary relinquishment of the boundary between subject and object. The individual, of course, is terrified of this, and his refusal to let go of its separateness is the primary obstacle to transcendence.

The vocabulary of transpersonal psychology, resembling as it does the vocabulary of many sacred traditions, requires that we examine its relationship to the sacred.[1] Such terms as "states of consciousness," "enlightenment," "freedom from the ego," and "self-realization" have their sources in the practical core of ancient sacred writings. When these words and ideas are employed by modern psychologists, the question arises as to whether they have similar meanings, since they come from two such different angles of approach. To understand ideas about the structure of the universe as expressed in sacred traditions requires first of all a change of perspective, in particular a receptivity to "ideas that help us to discover the truth for ourselves as opposed to concepts that organize what has already been discovered either by ourselves or others."[2] The tendency of many advocates of transpersonal psychology to use the methods of the meditative traditions either without engaging their metaphysics and cosmologies or by altering them to conform to the scientific paradigm suggests that this receptivity has yet to be achieved.

Method without Metaphysic

Abraham Maslow is among those who have attempted to restate the principles of the transpersonal experience without accepting the metaphysical assumptions of the sacred tradition that lies behind it. In Maslow's view, certain "being-values" (truth, wholeness, goodness, etc.) are revealed at moments of "peak experience," and these, far from being merely the subjective values of mystics, are objective, "real" qualities. These values "supply us with a perfectly naturalistic variety of 'certainty,' of unity, of eternity, of universality."[3] The person whose perception of these being-values is sufficiently acute realizes that they transcend sickness, pain, and death and can accept these evils: "From a godlike or Olympian point of view, all these are necessary, and can be understood as necessary."[4]

Thus we understand the world to be one because the world really *is* one. Why is it, then, that most of us, most of the time, fail to perceive it this way? Maslow's answer, and that of humanistic/transpersonal psychologies as a whole, has been to insist that whatever impedes us from achieving peak experience and perceiving the eternal values is accidental or incidental and can be overcome. Pain, rigidity, and ignorance are all correctable conditions; deficiencies in personality are common but can be transcended. Peak experiences may not become the normal continuous mode of consciousness for anyone, but the values and view of reality apprehended during peak experiences can be retained at all times. Maslow calls the person whose peak experiences are more frequent and better integrated into daily life, "self-actualized."

The primary culprit in keeping peak experiences from being noticed or respected is society, particularly as it manifests itself in bureaucratic institutions, which are permeated by a narrow, materialistic rationalism. One of these institutions is the scientific establishment, which, since the nineteenth century, has made life mechanical and value-free. Another enemy of mystical experience is organized religion, whose rulers, Maslow speculates, are "non-peakers" who seek to suppress peak experience out of fear.[5] Advocates of transpersonal psychologies often identify transcendental states with religious experience, and clearly, for many of Maslow's followers the core of religious experience is unitive, ineffable, and joyous; other aspects of religion are culturally conditioned localisms, devoid of religious or psychological interest. In the words of another transpersonal psychologist, Claudio Naranjo, "Religion is in autumnal foliage. The domain we discuss is within the roots, or within the ripening seed, in which the tree both begins and ends."[6] This candid lack of interest in ritual, myth, and public worship results in a concept of religious experience as an utterly privatized interior apprehension of a universal force.

The form of psychology Maslow and Naranjo practice has been characterized as "psychological religiousness."[7] No longer the enemy of religion, psychology has become a vehicle for a new form of religiousness, a new way to encounter the sacred and the ultimate. Psychological religiousness rejects the tradition and language that are so much a part of all externalized sacred rituals, and designates the innermost core of the person, the true self (as opposed to the helpless, bewildered ego of the ordinary personality) as the site at which the sacred manifests itself.[8] This self is seen as continuous with impersonal and universal beneficent forces that followers accept as characteristic of the cosmos. On these premises is based the promise of individual liberation and wholeness through harmony with the cosmos.

Psychological religiousness presents at least three positive aspects. First, it provides a badly needed context for encouraging people to identify with and trust their own experiences. Second, in spite of its occasionally trite and sentimental language, transpersonal psychology implicitly rejects the pervasive cultural need to dominate and manipulate both nature and the body, offering a vision of nonexploitive fulfillment for those who can no longer accept a concept of the universe as directed by personal forces. Third, the universalism of psychological religiousness—its attempt to focus on a transcultural core of mystical experience—explicitly accepts the idea that the world is one. This may have the beneficial effect of provoking the reexamination of the claims to truth made by particular religions. Psychological religiousness, by postulating a natural and nonrelative center within the self and the reality of a universal religious experience, may encourage fresh thought within traditional religious faiths.

At the same time, psychological religiousness suffers from serious deficiencies; for example, it fails to acknowledge the widespread ennui with the self and the world that manages to persist amid so much psychotherapy. Psychologists like Maslow do not acknowledge the immense and well-attested capacity of human beings for self-deception. It is at least possible that with an increased reliance on our own inner resources we are more likely to discover our own capacity for self-deception, but in the popular writing on inner experience, hardly any attention is given to this possiblity. As a consequence, even these psychologists' descriptions of the depths of the true self seem banal and shallow.

The second major failing of psychological religiousness lies in its negative assessment of religious traditions. Its emphasis on the primacy of inner experience results in an indifference to and ignorance of the past as a vital element capable of infusing the present with meaning. In fact, Maslow has gone so far as to declare that tradition not only is without value but actually acts as a barrier to the cultivation of one's own awareness.[9] In this statement, which implies that his own naturalistic religiousness, his investigations of peak experiences, his beliefs in being-values and self-actualization are without precedent and without antecedents, he exhibits a profound naiveté about the culture-laden nature of all experience. For it was the interpretive framework of natural religiousness that permitted his rediscovery of a mystical core of religious experience, and it is only this stance that allows him to determine which aspects of mystical accounts are "localisms" without real value and which genuinely provide insights into being. While Maslow's view of mystical experience intends to be naturalistic and culture-free, it is in fact determined by very specific cultural beliefs shared by many psychologists. Like the eighteenth century's quests for natural religion, this psychological search for a universal core to religion minimizes the role of culture in shaping all experience. But unlike the deists, whose natural religion took the form of specific propositions, the advocates of mysticism offer what is fundamentally an amorphous sense of the oneness of the self and the world. In a fragmenting and alienating environment, this may well provide some comfort, but can it live up to the expectations it elicits?

A third serious failing of the psychological religiousness movement lies in the fact that in placing all its emphasis on individual inner experience, it entirely devalues group membership. Group activities seem no more than expedient means to achieve private, individualized goals, and should they prove unsatisfactory or unnecessary, such activities are clearly dispensable. Establishing one's identity through inner experience is too delicate a process to be encumbered with permanent commitments to others, which could become burdensome. The strong tendency to reserve the private sphere as the realm of the authentic results in indifference to the public sphere, which becomes irrelevant, if not actually the object of mistrust. As various concerned sociologists have pointed out, when identity and the ultimate values are sought only in each person's private world, the great power and resources of the community are forgotten or ignored.[10] To make the depths of the individual self so attractive and redemptive is to privilege self-fulfillment over justice and charity; ironically, this preoccupation with the self is being promoted at precisely the moment when honoring our national moral obligations to the rest of the world is becoming more imperative than ever before.

Furthermore, it is clear that the self widely hailed by popular writers is not really the cosmic transcendent reality as described, for example, in the Upanishads (where the atman, or cosmic self, is said to be identical with the ultimate reality of Brahman). The self as it is conceived by transpersonal psychologists is little more than the empirical personality writ large and placed on center stage. Indeed, much literature on dying, in its discussion of the self, is clearly addressing only the ego and exalting its competence, rationality, and autonomy. Moving Western readers away from identification with the ego and toward a more cosmic conception of the Self will require more than capitalizing the word.

Death, Self, and Society

Retreat into the self cannot provide escape from the dilemma posed by the fearsome realities of human experience. With Dachau behind us, nuclear annihilation looming ahead of us, and our daily lives witnessing an explosion of violence, senseless death seems to loom in our past, our present, and our future. What are we to make of the paradox of knowing that thanks to medical science we may live longer than humans ever have—if we survive?[11] Moreover, our society juxtaposes a pornographic fascination with violent death with an insistence on treating actual death euphemistically and evasively. Much of the therapeutic response to death has, unfortunately, tended to ignore the experience of violent death, along with the fact that the Holocaust and Armageddon are inextricably a part of our image of death.

The publication in 1979 of Robert Jay Lifton's *The Broken Connection* marked the appearance of a new map of consciousness that directly addressed the cultural and personal implications of the threat of nuclear destruction. Rejecting the traditional psychoanalytical focus on the origins of disturbance rather than on experiential states, Lifton insists that symbols are not primarily defenses against reality. Instead, he contends that "the symbolic process around death and immortality" provides "the individual's experience of participation in some form of life continuity": "Images which suggest immortality reflect a compelling and universal quest for continuous symbolic relationship to what has gone before and what will continue after our finite individual lives. . . . The struggle toward, or experience of, a sense of immortality is in itself neither compensatory nor 'irrational' but an appropriate symbolization of our biological and historical connectedness."[12]

Thus the death of the individual should not be confused with the death of everything, and patterns of "symbolic immortality" help acknowledge continuities within nature, history, and the cosmos. Symbolic immortality is defined as "imagined (symbolized) perpetuation of the self through connection with larger forms of culture."[13] While the "I" will cease to exist, elements of the self and its impact on others will continue to exist, not as the self as such but as part of a human flow that absorbs and recreates the components of that impact to the point of altering their shape and obscuring their origin. Imagining this process contributes significantly to accepting death.

Lifton refuses to attribute the modern fear of death to human nature, looking instead to history for an explanation. Life in the modern era, particularly since the first use of nuclear weapons in 1945, has been lived on the brink of global catastrophe. Lifton notes, "As death imagery comes to take the shape of total annihilation or extinction, religious symbolism becomes both more sought after and more inadequate."[14] In the face of this threat, no "higher affirmation" has proven equal to the task, and the result has been a crumbling of confidence in all images of connectedness, such as family, community, and society. At fault is the false faith of nuclearism, an ideology that expresses itself in the hope that weapons themselves will bring peace and political transformation and will serve as a magic key to human mastery over nature. Moreover, according to Lifton, it is "the passionate embrace of nuclear weapons as a solution to death anxiety and a way of restoring a lost sense of immortality": "It involves a search for grace and glory in which technical-scientific transcendence, apocalyptic destruction, national power, personal salvation and committed individual identity become psychically bound up with the bomb."[15] The mythologies of the world are rich in apocalypses, and in Lifton's eyes such myths invite us to reassure ourselves that a new heaven and earth will emerge from the ruins of the old. The renunciation of nuclearism and of the false promise of a victory over death through mass killing becomes a moral imperative.

Lifton's trust in life, in the cycle of generations, and in people's capacity to integrate death experiences suggests a countermyth, that of the survivor. His work with survivors of Hiroshima and with Vietnam veterans suggests that "renewal involves a survivor experience: there is a measure of annihilation along with imagery of vitality beyond the death immersion."[16] This is a form of "ethical naturalism," but a very sophisticated one that gives priority to symbolizing capacities while rejecting an immortality severed from natural continuities and capacities. Lifton tries to affirm the connectedness that exists between world and soul, such that the inner person and the biological one are no longer at odds. Lifton sees our current state of affairs as an opportunity to renounce divisions and seek the nexus between the human and the natural, soul and earth, life and death.

Lifton's psychology deals with issues that many of the psychologies of inner experience fail to address. He is remarkable for his ethical sensitivity, his recognition of the importance of culture and history, and his more unitary view of the nature of human beings. It is this unitary view that permits moral outrage, not on the behalf of the heroic ego or the inner depths of the soul, but in the name of threatened humanity.

Transcendence and Sacred Tradition

The transpersonal psychologies we have been examining have drawn heavily, though selectively, on humanity's ancient sacred traditions. Yet as John H. Crook has pointed out, many of the elements of the sacred traditions have changed radically in the hands of psychologists. Meditation, for example, in most of its secular manifestations, has become goal-oriented, a means to relaxation and better health. It has also become an essentially intellectual and individual activity of a tension-ridden society, a society whose malaise arises precisely from the individual's alienation from the spiritual and the communal.

Advocates of the transformative rather than the therapeutic experience argue that it is not enough to be religiously moved. What is needed is a conscious relationship to the spiritual event. For Christ's disciples, for example, the initial encounter with the risen Christ was at first deeply disturbing and incomprehensible. They were excited, not enlightened, and the startling event had to be assimilated and connected with previous experiences and ideas. This kind of assimilation requires an entirely new frame of reference, larger, more comprehensive, and more in keeping with the new experience. Thus the conscious integration of religious experience involves the world of meaning and ideas, as well as its vehicle, language.

Those who seek transformation within one of the world's ancient sacred traditions tend to have difficulty accepting certain of that tradition's precepts regarding, for example, resurrection or the structure of the universe. These ideas often appear to be founded on inconsistencies and expressed in images guaranteed to confuse or offend the more "reasonable" side of our nature. On the whole, we prefer ideas that offer intellectually or emotionally satisfying explanations. Yet some ideas are meant to be something other than explanations. They are, as Needleman expresses it, "ideas that help one to discover the truth for oneself,"[17] and these are what we have been calling "sacred" or "cosmic." Their function is entirely different from that of the teachings religion intends to promote human external well-being. They are systems of ideas that expose, then unify our fragmented and warring inner nature, and it is only within the controlled conditions offered by the "path" that the ideas, symbols, sacred writings, and patterns of living can work together to produce transformation.

There is a sense of wonder that accompanies the realization that there are different levels of existence in the universe and in ourselves. Unfortunately, the sense of wonder has become mixed with egotism, and, having discovered the multileveled nature of the universe, we tend to dream of striding from one level to the next, eliminating the differences, when in fact we need to open ourselves to the higher levels and allow them to guide us to our unknown selves. In order for this to happen, we need the paths offered by religious tradition, paths that present ideas in ways that circumvent the interference of the ego and intellect.

"All around us, both within and outside of the sciences, there is a yearning to heal the fragmentations and divisions that separate man from nature, man from man, and man from God."[18] To Needleman's list, we might add the yearning to heal the rift between humanity and death. The search for new, unifying concepts of the universe and the social order has begun.

Reshaping Death

Our current inability to confront death began when Christianity ceded to science the exclusive right to make pronouncements on the nature of the cosmos. As the scale of the known universe was reduced by scientific metaphysics, so was the scale of the unknown, of death. No longer an abstraction on a cosmic scale, death has come to mean only individual death. Death just means *my* death, and it preoccupies us without compelling us to admit our ignorance of ourselves and of the world we inhabit. Lost in the illusion that we stand over against the entire universe, we now assume that we can come to terms with death merely by thinking about it, by finding the right scientific, psychological, or religious categories with which to explain our relationship with it. But no relationship with death is possible as long as we take death so personally that we reduce cosmic law to the scale of our own ego. What ideas can allow us to contemplate death, the mere prospect of which sends the ego into fits of sentimentality, in tenaciously held beliefs that comfort the ego; of despair, in intellectual systems that glorify anxiety; and of defiance, ensconced in a fortress of science and technology? How can the inevitability of our own deaths be used to galvanize a search for a more fundamental reality in the self?

First must come the perception of the universe as a great system of consciousness, which can lead to the awareness that death can do no more than frighten the ego. Yet ideas alone cannot remake our attitudes toward death; our ideas have notoriously little impact on how we actually live our lives. These ideas, says Needleman, must enter the body.[19] One way for this to happen is through physical or emotional suffering, perhaps through the death of a loved one or when our own lives are in danger. Such an experience, by lending concreteness to the concept of death, may prove an awakening force. At these moments, we tend to see ourselves sharply, and to realize that the self we see is not the only one we possess. There is something more, something we have never been in touch with before that is nonetheless intensely familiar.

From encounters with death springs a metaphysics, a view of reality and of human nature that is not normally accessible to us in our everyday state of consciousness. Is it possible, then, to create an experience similar to death, within the scale of our individual existence, that can help us discover something of the truth of death while remaining in our habitual state of consciousness? Can there be any experience analogous to death that does not simply reduce it to the habitual terms of the domineering ego? In some traditions, the search for this kind of experience is called "conscious dying."[20] Many sacred works that prescribe conduct for the dying, such as *The Tibetan Book of the Dead*,[21] may also be understood as guides for the living in the search for truth. What sacred traditions have referred to—in language often no longer understood—as the separation of body and soul at the moment of death is an analogy for the separation of pure awareness from ordinary consciousness. It is in this state of "freedom from clinging to thought—where an important thought is allowed to move on, to disappear, forever beyond recall—that one may have an experience analogous to that

of death, which is the disappearance of one's self."[22] The experience
of actually facing death cannot be counterfeited, but we can recreate it
in miniature to the extent that the experience permits the birth of a new
consciousness.

Of course, each of us must verify this claim for ourselves, and this
is not as simple as it may sound. In the literature of spiritual psychology, the art of separating oneself from thought is always associated
with perfect stillness of the body, which is held in a precise balance
between relaxation and tension. Furthermore, this rather difficult discipline can be effective only when applied within the framework of a
system of ideas, with a strong relationship to a guide and a community,
and with an attitude toward life that must be learned and diligently
practiced.

We as a culture desperately need to be able to face the reality of
death and to come to terms with its meaning. Yet it should be clear
that we cannot rethink our relationship to death without rethinking
our relationship to the cosmos. It is precisely this relationship that the
earth's sacred traditions have always addressed, and not merely in
their methods but also in their metaphysics and their cosmologies.

Death and the Christian Faith

Transpersonal thought in the West has found much of its stimulus in
such Eastern religions as Hinduism, Buddhism, and Islam, whose "oth-
erness" is surely part of their appeal. Ironically, the Christian meditative tradition has attracted far less attention. In examining the elements
of the Christian tradition that compose the sacred path, I hope to correct some distortions of that tradition that have contributed significantly to the destructive forces in Western culture. As Bishop Leslie
Newbigin has noted, the greatest missionary challenge of our time is
the "conversion of the pagan West."[23]

The meditative traditions of both the Christian West and the Christian East are intensely experiential. The Christian East, in particular,
has rejected the distinction between academic theology and personal
spirituality. Far from being an academic exercise, theology is an encounter with the living God, and must be nourished with sacramental
worship, solitude, pastoral care, and the healing of souls. In the Christian meditative tradition, theology must arise from and remain involved with human experience on earth.

> There is . . . no Christian mysticism without theology; but above all, there is no
> theology without mysticism. . . .

It is an existential attitude which involves the whole man: There is no theology apart from the experience; it is necessary to change, to become a new man. To know God one must draw near to him. No one who does not follow the path of union with God can be a theologian.[24]

Christian mysticism of this sort should not be mistaken for a re-treat from our responsibility to the world. A theology whose central motif is a crucifixion cannot avoid the issues of suffering and death. In fact it is this gospel of death, bringing home both the tragedy and the joyfulness of life, that has always constituted the appeal of the Chris-tian Gospel. The life and death of Jesus Christ has always allowed Christians to make sense of both, mingling pessimism about life with optimism about God and the hope for life in God.

People rarely die the rather idealized deaths many thanatologists choose to contemplate, and psychologies of death have failed, more often than not, to address the meaning of the suffering that usually accompanies death in the real world. The psychoanalytically inclined have tended to respond with stoicism; the humanistic, existential thinkers often stray into romantic naturalism. Robert Jay Lifton and the Jungians concentrate instead on the processes of imaging and symbol-izing people use to raise the prospect and meaning of death to cosmic dimensions.

All sacred traditions, on the other hand, have grappled with the meaning of human suffering, and this struggle has always been a hall-mark of Christian thinking. Symbols of what Paul Tillich called the power of "nonbeing,"[25] of suffering and moral pain, occur in many of the world's religions: in Christianity, the cross; in Judaism, exile; in Buddhism, samsara (the totality of the world as suffering). The under-lying structure of reality is perceived to be estrangement from God and the dominion of death, and the divine appears fully enmeshed in the fundamental discontinuity and pain of all things. Far from signifying that the world is bad and human existence meaningless, such symbols proclaim the presence of God and the possibility of liberation even when all seems lost. Yet no condition of blessedness or eventual libera-tion denies the power and reality of these symbols, which represent a near-ultimate negativity in the world of humans, in the inner self, and in the very structure of the universe.

The power of nonbeing has long been a focus of Christian mysti-cism. In the mystic tradition of the fourth and fifth centuries, the spiri-tual path led literally through the desert, where neither mankind nor nature could offer comfort, and where prayer must address God in faith. It is here, notes Thomas Merton, that "the monk is bound to explore the inner waste of his own being as a solitary."[26] The goal of the Desert Fathers was to develop the "single eye" through which one "sees God" when reality is stripped of the illusion of the ego's centrality.[27]

The desert tradition, however bizarrely its radical asceticism may strike us today, was not the only one to have sought God in desolation. The Christian mystics of the fourteenth and fifteenth centuries sought enlightenment in the depths of darkness and despair. In the words of the fourteenth-century German mystic, Meister Eckhart, "the ground of the soul is dark,"[28] yet he urges us not to flee from this truth but to use it as an avenue to find God. An anonymous English contemporary, the author of *The Cloud of Unknowing*, describes the search for God as an experience of torturing doubt and sorrow. The soul, in its efforts to penetrate the cloud of unknowing, where it would hold fellowship with God, is constantly thwarted by the consciousness of its own being—the earthly, sensual, rebellious part of its nature: "And yet in all this sorrow he desireth not to unbe: for that were devil's madness and despite unto God. But he liketh right well to be; and he giveth full heartily thanks unto God, for the unworthiness and gift of his being, although he desire unceasingly for to lack the knowing and the feeling of his being."[29]

Spanish mystics of the sixteenth century also testified to the centrality of symbols of nonbeing on the path to God. Imprisoned in Toledo, St. John of the Cross said, "Abandonment is a file and the endurance of darkness leads to great light."[30] His contemporary St. Teresa of Avila wrote at length on the experience of nonbeing in the next-to-last dwelling place of the soul before its union with God: "I tell you there is need for more courage than you think."[31]

Each of these mystical traditions insists on the necessity of the death of the self before achieving union with the divine, and, inevitably, the experiences in question entail suffering. These experiences are analogous to the experience of death and may consequently prepare us for that ultimate loss of ego that occurs at the end of life.

The Christian faith's understanding of death has been succinctly charted by Jaroslav Pelikan, who uses five geometric figures to illustrate the concepts of death developed by five fathers of the early Church: The arc of existence denotes the finality of death; the circle of immortality represents the analogy between human life and the eternal life of God; the triangle of mortality reminds that even if the soul is immortal, the person must die to God and receive life from God; the parabola of eternity indicates that death is God's way of bringing the soul back to himself; and the spiral of history insists that the death of the individual cannot be understood except in relation to the deaths of Adam and of Christ.

Pelikan uses the figure of the cross to summarize these thoughts. Signed with the cross at baptism, the believer is signed with it again at death, thus it symbolizes the arc of existence. The cross also emblematizes the disclosure of something mysterious in the heart of God, his capacity to know the meaning of human suffering and death. Thus, like the circle of immortality but far more profoundly, the cross describes the analogy between the life of humanity and the eternal life of God. The cross also represents the death of one who lived for God alone and who died in unbroken unity with God, who received life from God and was raised from the dead to the glory of God the Father. Thus the cross brings together, more definitively than the triangle of mortality, the horizontal and vertical lines in the shape of death. Jesus died on the cross but was raised again to receive a kingdom that has no end. Thus the cross defines both the lowest point and the origin and destiny of the parabola of eternity. Finally, the spiral of history, as well, is reflected in the symbol of the cross, for the figure on it is the second Adam, who went into the Garden of Gethsemane to save those who had been expelled from the Garden of Eden. All in all, the conception of death within the Christian faith is meant to make it possible to live in courage and die in dignity, for while mankind may know little of the contours of the undiscovered country, it does know that by the grace of the cross, Christ changed the shape of death.[32]

Certainly there has been much banality in Christian thought about death, but there are also profoundly meaningful contemporary accounts of "death in Christ." Lay theologian William Stringfellow reflects upon the death of his companion, Anthony Towne:

> Anthony had, long since, suffered whatever the power of death and the fear or thrall of the power of death could do to him through alcoholism, and, in that suffering, he had encountered the grace of the Word of God, enabling him to transcend that suffering. . . . Having already died in Christ, his self-hood had been rescued, established, identified, fulfilled, and finished, so that his death, while poignant, was not waste or tragedy or demonic triumph or incentive to despair. In traditional syntax, Anthony had found his life in his loss of life in Christ.[33]

Stringfellow's interpretation of his friend's adjustment to death (through having experienced it before actually dying) recalls Needleman's suggestion that we seek experiences analogous to death in preparation for it. The experience of nonbeing is deathlike, and its redemptive nature resides in the fact that it allows us to perceive the cosmos as comprising multiple realities, not just that of metaphysical empiricism. As a result, we can detach ourselves from the cause of suffering and, by focusing on that which lies beyond suffering, we achieve a sense of wholeness and unity with all creation. The final product of this deepened sense of the self in relation to God is a sense of renewal—having passed through the deathlike experience and the reordering of life, we can live as freer and more loving people.

An essential aspect of the deathlike experience of mystical prayer is that, appearances to the contrary notwithstanding, it is not a solitary, individualized endeavor. In fact, the process by which the individual and the human community are made one by the divine is at the heart of sacred teachings. The shepherd and his flock are a major motif in the New Testament, and this social dimension of spirituality is crucial, especially given its omission from many psychologies of inner experience. The Christian is not seeking a solitary walk with God, a private mystical trip, the flight of the alone to the Alone. Instead, he or she is part of a corporate search for humanity, renewal, and the Kingdom of God—the cosmos. The mystical traditions insist on this, and anyone who seeks to carry on the spiritual quest outside of this context runs serious risks. The world's great spiritual teachers have spoken as one in warning of the dangers of a search for enlightenment that ignores common humanity, the human community, and the demands of justice and peace.

5

Commitment and Community
in the Face of Death

Pastoral theology, if it is to be able to guide the dying, must directly confront the underlying cultural causes that have made dying a fearsome process and death a reality we can no longer acknowledge. At the same time, it must seriously examine how theology itself has been guilty of complicity in the entrenchment of death-denial, knowingly or unknowingly appropriating some of the same secular values and assumptions that have reinforced our culture's terror of death. Among these are the preoccupation with technology, which has led us to think of death as just another malfunction to be fixed, nuclearism, a "tyranny of survival" that none of us may survive, and radical individualism, which accompanies the fragmentation of community.

The Dualistic Model

Western society has broken radically with its religious past, and with the advent of secularism, belief in the immortality of the soul has lost much of its power to comfort the dying. Christian theologians from the Church Fathers through the reformers of the sixteenth century had taken for granted the immortality of the soul and believed as well in the resurrection of the body.[1] In the eighteenth and nineteenth centuries, belief in an afterlife, though somewhat modified, remained a powerful force.[2] Today, however, many philosophers, as well as psychologists and social critics, dismiss the possibility of life after death.[3] Existentialists have opposed belief in an afterlife as a distraction from the most essential task of human authenticity—apprehension of our own finitude and mortality. Even modern biblical scholars have rejected the concept of life after death, distinguishing between the primitive Christian hope for the resurrection of the body and the Hellenic-idealist doctrine of the immortality of the soul.

Josef Pieper rejects the use of visions of immortality as a panacea for the dying, since such answers suggest that "at bottom . . . man does not really 'die' at all," but only the body dies.[4] He roundly attacks the "spiritualistic minimalizing" that separates immortal soul from perishing body.[5] Pieper argues that, contrary to this dualistic simplification, death claims the whole person, body and soul.[6] Yet in spite of his attempt to admit some darkness into the death chamber by admitting that death violently interrupts and destroys the "forming of the body . . . contrary to the innermost intention of the soul and of man himself,"[7] Pieper's own system employs a dualism that does not permit him to speak of the death of the whole person. He first replaces the terms "person" and "whole man" with "soul," allowing him to argue finally that the soul, "although profoundly affected by death, nevertheless persists indestructibly and maintains itself, remains in being."[8] Pieper's "nevertheless" determines the ultimate course of his discussion, which becomes a denial that death is a pervasive, personal threat. The soul survives death untouched, watching the body's collapse from its immortal vantage point. By using terms like "man himself" as addenda (if not simple synonyms) for "soul," Pieper guides his whole discussion away from the dark. His model allows for no serious exploration of death as an appalling prospect, always insinuating instead an affirmative note that amounts, in the end, to a denial of darkness and a persistent apologia for immortality.

Karl Rahner's work represents a more serious theological venture into the darker realms. For Rahner, the classic definition of death, while neither false nor unjustified on its own terms, is seriously limited by its failure to admit that death is "an event for man as a whole and as a spiritual person."[9] Theology can no longer consider death as something that "affects only the so-called body of man, while the so-called soul . . . [is] able to view the fate of its former partner . . . unaffected and undismayed as from above."[10] Death affects the whole person, including the soul. The dualistic model, by freeing the immortal soul so easily from the grip of death, offers a definition of death that is both intellectually and affectively thin. Rahner makes explicit what Pieper demonstrates by default—that the body-soul model prevents a full-fledged exploration of the dark aspects of death. By suggesting that the darkness is more apparent than real (since only the dispensable body is mortal), this paradigm represents, ultimately, a refusal to take death seriously or confront it directly.

The Natural Model

Many of theology's "natural" or "life-cycle" models of death also prove inadequate in their reductionism. Again, the devastation caused by death becomes merely a surface phenomenon, an ambiguous outer dimension that can be "seen through" and eventually dissolved. Life-cycle models emphasize that death is an entirely natural event and an inescapable part of life, one that can be made tolerable by openly and courageously seizing life on its own terms. Such is the model found in the work of Robert E. Neale, who raises theological issues in spite of his basically psychological approach.[11] Like Kübler-Ross, Neale focuses on the psychological conflicts that have made the prospect of death an unspeakable obstacle to imagination, affectivity, and human sharing. He makes it clear that fears of death are deeply rooted, densely tangled, and not easily unwound, but his purpose is to identify and dispel them, releasing us from fear and silence. Yet although Neale strives to address death head on, behind his therapy lurks the conviction that the darkness surrounding death is a shadow cast by psychic failure, and that death itself is not dark. His schema requires first that we acknowledge our fears, then that we dispel them through the realization that they have been engendered not by death but by life.[12] The apparent terrors that await in death are simple misperceptions that betray personal resentment of the nature of life and an immature determination to hold on defiantly. Once we have identified our distorted life-patterns, they can be challenged and corrected, and fears of death are overcome in the process, for a life that has been fully accepted will culminate in a "finely finished death."[13]

In the final analysis, Neale's psychological interpretation mediates the dark aspects of death, transforming them into the flawed products of individual psychic histories. Neale himself acknowledges the danger of this approach, which is that it trivializes death and reduces its threatening aspects to the tics and quirks of human personality. Nonetheless, he fails to respond to his own criticism, and his fundamental assumption—that the terrors and incomprehensibility of death are apparent rather than real—remains unaltered. The fear of death is still just a reflection of inner failures and inadequacies, indicating an inability to accept natural change and rebirth into the unknown. Acceptance models like Neale's articulate a paradigm that theology can draw upon without risking any real confrontation with the meaning of death, which becomes the last rhythm of life, the climactic move into the new and the unknown. Immortality, in some form, is only a breath away.

An acceptance model that blends easily with belief in immortality and can be readily incorporated into theology is that of Roger Troisfon-taines.[14] He envisions each human life in terms of two natural curves—the downward curve of the body, whose powers diminish with age, and the upward curve of the spirit, whose potential never ceases to grow. The two trajectories, while countervailing, are not equal, for the upward curve of the soaring spirit plots the truly significant line of life and offers the essential clue to the meaning of death. The upward journey of each person's spirit imposes

> a forever-binding obligation to tear himself away, willingly or reluctantly, from an environment where his equilibrium [is] more passive, more external, and to enter into a vast, more complex new situation, where he is bound to fail unless he enters deeper and deeper into his own self and is united ever more intimately to the being he discovers step by step.[15]

All meaningful human growth, in these terms, is a "tearing away" from a set of external circumstances that have "become like so many prisons."[16] In the course of life, the spirit progresses primarily through a series of separations, of dislodging births. Death is merely the most dramatic of these, the climactic surge of growth whereby the body gives birth to the person.

> As the butterfly leaves the cocoon where it has developed as a chrysalis, as the fetus breaks the amnion at birth, so also, when we step into the final state of our destiny, we leave this body which has been the primary condition of our personal ripening.[17]

> When the umbilical cord breaks at the moment of birth, a new, vast horizon opens out. It will continue to expand. This earthly body, this placenta of the spiritual person, is a nourishing as well as a restrictive agent. It will be abandoned insofar as it means limitation; as a result, the soul will find that its relationship with the world becomes easier and more universal. Death enlarges our situation "indefinitely."[18]

The falling curve of bodily energy ceases to chart a course relevant to human experience, while the rising curve of spiritual development becomes the unique indicator of meaning. In the end, Troisfontaines's model transforms death into an event more fetal than fearsome, and with unblinking optimism it is seen as sensible and heartening, posing no challenge whatsoever to religious faith and theological systems.

In its reductive positivism, Troisfontaines's view of death is in keeping with Neale's. Like the classical body-soul model, it purports to resolve the problem of death by revealing its "inner meaning," and it finds that meaning to be consistent with the values and verities of

life. Clearly, the acceptance of death such theories promote is thera-
peutically desirable. But if "acceptable death" becomes the single nor-
mative possibility, then theology has fixed its gaze on the ideal deaths
that people should die, rather than on the grim deaths many people
suffer through in the real world.

Death as the Final Decision

Neale's psychological model envisions death anxiety in terms of psychic integrity and the ability to confront and accept mortality. A com-
parable approach in philosophy would elevate acceptance from a psychic attitude to an essential anthropological attribute, from a psychological possibility to a metaphysical property. Death ceases to be something that happens to us and becomes instead the central inner act
whereby we accept and affirm ourselves. Death's power, in this context, is neither alien nor intrusive but a personal and fulfilling experience in which we seek authentic existence and which gives life its
ultimate shape.

   Ladislaus Boros has developed this kind of "final option" model,
in which death is "man's first completely personal act, and is, therefore, by reason of its being, the place above all others for the awakening
of consciousness, for freedom.... "[19] His paradigm depends on an
anthropological scheme that focuses on the incompleteness of human
life and on the idea that in all the central areas of human existence—
knowledge, volition, self-awareness, affectivity—we are limited by the
inherently transitory and partial nature of our actions.[20] The only finality is that offered by death, which breaks the stuttering pattern of finitude: "The first integral act of knowing will be possible for us only in
the moment of death."[21] Death is the only opportunity we will ever
have to decisively shape ourselves and achieve the self-integration that
the transitory nature of life has always denied us. It is the moment
when the deepest levels of the person are fused and freed from the
mutable, ever-shifting patterns of life.

   This final-option view defines death in terms of finality, comple-
tion, and release from time's fragmentary modes, which are "mere"
process and possibility. Boros does not reject outright that death has its
painful and destructive aspects, but his paradigm implicitly relegates
these to positions of secondary importance: "I am being carried away
to where I have always been in my dreams, in my longings, to that
region which I have always divined behind things, persons,/ and
events.... Everything merges into one, marvelously radiant...."[22]
Though this deliriously joyful vision should be consoling, Boros's

model is curiously uncomforting. After all, if the philosophically critical moment of death is the only time that decisions have meaning,
what value is there in a lifetime's worth of struggles and difficult decisions? The prospect of death is made palatable by denigrating life.

The glorification of death in final-option models is consistent with
much traditional theology, which has tended to depict it as a super-
mystical moment standing in shining contrast to the flawed history and
poor stuff of life. In choosing this stance, theology has opted not to
address death's truly frightening aspects.

Karl Rahner has made an attempt to correct the distorting extremes
to which the final-option model has been carried. While he describes
death as an integrating decision, he refuses to dismiss the reality of the
darker aspects of death, which he calls the "radical spoliation" of
humanity, "destruction, a rupture, an accident which strikes man from
without, unforeseeable...."[23] Death offers for our contemplation its
own "empty, unsubstantial, uncanny character" before which the human creature shrinks in horror.[24] The dark elements are not peripheral
surface qualities that will dissolve before the knowing gaze, but aspects
rooted in the unity of person and nature and in the interpenetration of
freedom and fate.

It is the inescapable tension between choice and constraint, between the freedom of the individual and the ineluctable determination
of the world that is, for Rahner, the primary principle of human existence. From this tension develops a dialectic in which each of us experiences both the malleability and intransigence of life, the pathos of
an external fate running counter to personal choice and meaning. This
pathos is, of course, most intense when one is dying and must watch
self-determination succumb to nature, and we sink into a passivity
that is not merely corporeal but envelops the entire being. This holistic
perception is in keeping with Rahner's criticism of interpretations of
death that cheerfully send the body to the grave while whisking the
soul off to eternal life. Rahner never speaks of the soul's freedom and
the body's fate or of the soul's activity and the body's passivity. Instead
he is always careful to speak in terms of the whole person's freedom
and fate. Besides refusing dualistic solutions, he avoids the terms of
the acceptance model and neither reduces death's dreadfulness to psychological defects and misperceptions nor rehabilitates death as birth
in disguise. Moreover, unlike Boros, Rahner does not restrict himself
to the final-option categories of freedom and act, and he postulates no
final, unencumbered, and liberating decision.

Nonetheless, Rahner argues predominantly in favor of the "active"
side of death. He is far more ready to acknowledge the frightening

aspects of death than the other theorists considered here, but he uses death's darker side primarily as a methodological check on a system that, in the final analysis, veers toward a positive interpretation of death. He may describe the humiliating passivity of death, but he also, and more insistently, describes it as "an active consummation from within brought about by the person himself, a maturing self-realization which embodies the result of what man has made of himself during life, the achievement of total self-possession, a real effectuation of self, the fulness of a freely produced personal reality."[25] For Rahner the essential dynamic for resolving the confrontation with death arises as the dialectic between inner action and outer passivity reaches for some final statement of meaning. We cannot know what that statement will be for any given person, for it is buried deep within. But while our deaths as individuals remain opaque, in Rahner's view death itself, in universal terms, is illuminated, a fulfilling event in which each of us, by confronting the terms of life's collapse, "brings the total result of his life's activity to its final state."[26] The tension between personal act and impersonal fate becomes itself the locus of freedom, which results from the stance we take in response to it. This death is ultimately declarative, not interrogative; it is a climactic expression of what it means to be fully and finally human.

Rahner's model finally comes down to another definition of the "good death," reminiscent of the acceptance models: "When a man dies patiently and humbly, when death itself is seen and accepted, when it not merely 'happens' in the course of striving for something else, and when perhaps death is not envisaged through blind eagerness for something (flight from shame, something obstinately sought, etc.), when death is loved for its own sake, and explicitly, it cannot but be a good death."[27] There is a methodological bias against dealing with the disabling aspects of death, its assault on order and explication. The model's noetic terms inherently abhor death's lack of sense. Both Rahner and Boros share the conviction that death is a locus of meaning and the answer to its own question, and consequently their models provide a convenient point of departure for theological reflection. But because their conviction seems impervious, if not oblivious, to the horrors that often really do accompany death, their models prove relentlessly affirmative.

An Art of Dying for a Dark Time

If theology wishes seriously to engage the challenge death poses, it will have to explore the full range of possible approaches and divest itself of a symbiotic dependency on a variety of models that provide it with only cheerful perspectives. There is no particular reason, other than wishful thinking, why death must always be seen as friendly to humans. Theology must balance its penchant for positive models by seriously considering models of death that accept it as something tangled and alien, that resists being explained away with final options or immortality. A theology moving in this direction would need an austere model of death and would have to be impatient with benign depictions, idealized scenarios, and attempts to reveal death's underlying logic. Rather than offering up deep secrets, such a theology could offer to thanatology a simple reminder that death is an ever-present rebuttal of human understanding. From beginning to end, a dark model would present death as relentless and implacable, a disintegration rather than an achievement, the final demonstration of human weakness and of the weakness of religious faith and theological articulation. With such a model, theology would be drawn into desperate and grievous struggle.

The advantage of a dark model of death is that it presses theology to cast off assumptions that would make of God a *deus ex machina* in the face of death. From the dark perspective, death is simply a block of silence, and the only solace theology can offer is faith in God. Instead of sweeping explanations of that which is, after all, unknowable, we receive a heightened sense of God's mystery, a sense that is not articulated as a conclusion but rather revealed and grasped only in the struggle with death. Death gives faith no theistic clues. Its featureless surface offers nothing to cling to and no source of comfort. Faith, then, simply waits for God to be God, on God's terms, in a freedom beyond all human understanding and experience. This is not a mystery to be sentimentalized; it is a realization of transcendence shaped by the *via negativa* and by the admission that human understanding is baffled by death, that argument and analysis, language and imagination are utterly inadequate. The dark model stresses that faith has no option but to enter the realm of death hoping that even here God will be God and that the apparent void will not be the only truth. It is a matter of waiting for the mystery of God to declare itself. It is a wait that has more in common with the dark night of the soul described by the mystics than with the near-death experiences of popular literature.

Besides urging upon theology a fresh approach to the question of God's transcendence, the dark model offers a new perspective on the question of God's immanence. This arises from its Christological ramifications—in other words, the significance of Jesus's death as bleak and emptying. Only when death is perceived as unrelieved dark and without inherent meaning does the death of Jesus become theologically meaningful. At the moment of human collapse, when there is only choked and beaten silence, faith dares to declare the presence of God. In the death of Jesus, the awful blankness of death is juxtaposed with the wholly Other. Faith cannot deny death's darkness but understands that Jesus died a difficult human death, the forsaken end that he feared and prayed about in the garden and cried out against while on the cross.

Focusing on Jesus's death, theology is forced to struggle with the issue of God's passion to understand the human condition on its own terms, even to the point of death. Thus a dark model nourishes a Christology constructed "from below," one that is rooted in the humanity of Jesus, and searches out revelations of God in all the forms of human history, even in the ragged edge of life that we call death. From this perspective, the death of Jesus cannot be understood simply as an act of expiation for sin and does not lend itself to any such manageable or schematically human explanation. It is instead a paradox for faith, the descent of God to the nothingness of human death.

God's immanence within death's emptiness is indescribable and inconceivable, yet this is precisely what the death of Jesus proclaims. God has entered into the fear of the dying body, the dreaded slipping away from others and from oneself, the slide into the terrifying unknown. Theology must struggle to determine what it means to have faith in a God who does not hold back from the godlessness of death, a condition that offers no proof of faith's validity or God's existence. This binds God to the place of faith's greatest difficulty. Moreover, it demands that theology wrestle with the fractious nature of God's immanence, His participation in the event of utter removal. Mystery is the primary mode of faith, but it is not a mystery that can be used as a master key or catchword for relieving the tension. Faith holds to a God whose closeness is never simply apparent or held in the grasp of human experience.

The resurrection of Jesus is the primal clue theology has to work from as it struggles to confront the issues raised by a dark vision of death. Theology must acknowledge, however, that the resurrection is not an a priori proposition that can be accepted as true. Instead, it is a claim as unverifiable as death is unknowable. Consequently, the resurrection does not dissipate the darkness and replace it with a luminous vision of death as sensible and meaningful. It is precisely because death appears to obviate human experience and the possibility of God that the resurrection stands as such a shocking counterclaim.

Faith looks to the resurrection of Jesus as the promise that God will be God even in the nullity that no human experience can breach.

Jesus does not remain in the web of death, and seen from within the context of the dark model, this is astounding, as it should be. God presents us with a paradox, a promise about human experience that violates everything human experience tells us. It is a message that counters death without in the least altering it. The resurrection of Jesus asks the human mind and the human heart to venture into the void armed only with faith, and at the same time, it makes humanity gasp in hope. Within the dark model, no ray of light penetrates the cloud of death. Instead, it is the nature of faith that is illuminated, as we see it as a reaching out that defies what we know as logic and relies upon the paradoxical word spoken in the death and resurrection of Jesus.

These theological repercussions begin to suggest how a dark model of death might inform care for the dying. Its value lies in its acknowledgment of what is disharmonic in human experience. The struggle of faith with these discordancies can become a descent into intellectual and spiritual barrenness, a journey into loss and lament. It is the journey Needleman describes as necessary if experiential knowledge is to enter the body and permeate the being. It also resembles the transcendent path of the Christian mystical tradition. Christian tradition is replete with such images of nonbeing as self-denial, suffering, and death, which can enable us to abandon images of self and of God until we are confronted with a God beyond the one constructed in the human mind. Scripture and tradition affirm that there lies in this process a fundamentally ineffable experience, hinted at through words like "resurrection" and "new creation."

These experiences have nothing in common with "peak experiences" or with the "good" and "acceptable" deaths proffered by the various elements, whether psychologically or religiously oriented, of the thanatology movement. While the movement's sensitivity has surely eased the end for many, we need the dark model's influence to correct the movement's tendency to both romanticize and secularize death. It is time to admit that many people, through no fault of their own, simply do not die ideal deaths; instead they die violently, or painfully, or too soon. It is also time to acknowledge that the resolution of intrapersonal conflicts, even assuming circumstances allow it, is not a response to the questions posed by the unknowable. Though these concerns are important, there remains in the dying a hunger for redemption and an eagerness for transcendence, and if these needs are to be met, we must turn to the sacred tradition.

A dozen years ago, at my mother's deathbed, she told me that she wished that God would let go of her. I was disconcerted by this apparent statement of doubt from a woman of great faith, but because I was afraid she was too weak to clarify what she meant, I did not press her to explain. Instead, I responded with the heartfelt, but too confident, assurance that God would never let go of her. I realize now that her words did not indicate a lack of faith at all, but rather a desire to move on to a goal beyond the pain and suffering that had been her lot for many weeks. I could have responded more appropriately by asking her to tell me more about God's letting go, and by acknowledging my own reluctant willingness to let her go. What I had interpreted as meaning abandonment may have implied instead a move toward a more comprehensive vision of life as including death. Of course, I can never know precisely what she meant. What I can understand now is that redemption and transcendence do not belong only to calm and bliss, but can be born as well of suffering and sorrow.

Obviously, this story is as much about me as about my mother, whose words filled me with anxiety. I hope that I have arrived at a greater understanding now, an understanding that has grown from her suffering, her faith, and her death, and from my suffering, my faith, and my confrontation with my own mortality.

We have no idea of what awaits beyond death, and speculation is essentially futile. We can, however, consider the consequences of affirming the hope of resurrection. The hope of resurrection produces a kind of survivorship that has been tempered in the fires of self-discipline, self-denial, and suffering. Many of the survivors of this century's greatest instances of both death and survival—the Holocaust and Hiroshima—have emerged from their encounter with the terrors of finitude with the desire to share with others their discoveries. Elie Wiesel, tempted by suicide, realized that he had not yet given his testament to the horrors of the living death he had experienced in the Holocaust: "That was a compelling reason—not to live but to survive."[28] Survivorship is an "art of dying" that can counter the reductionist, secular, romantic, and hedonistic emphases of some of the therapies we have examined. Unlike the "tyranny of survival," it does not value survival at any cost, grasping frantically for technological means to escape death. It is instead an expression of hope that can be born of the confrontation with symbols of nonbeing, one that sets the importance of human life in its proper context. It comes from facing death and reflecting on our own mortality, while yet struggling to survive. It allows us to realize that the love that causes our grief is the same as the love that furnishes our hope, that the love that makes us cry out in pain at the loss of human life also permits us an ultimately liberating intimacy with our dissolution.

An Ethic of Commitment

The experience of suffering and the glimpsed possibility of resurrection cannot be redemptive until we have moved beyond the attempt to make sense of individual experience and toward a compassion that expresses itself as a concern for justice. Any Christian experience unaccompanied by this concern for community is untrue to the biblical and historical Christian tradition. Those who would care for the dying must remain aware of the hazards of that rampant individualism that has resulted in the mantle of invisibility our culture has tried to cast over death. Faulty thinking about the self has led to faulty thinking about social rules, and one of the consequences is that we as individuals have often failed to develop a social ethic to replace the eroding ethic of self-denial. As Daniel Yankelovich notes, "The rhetoric of self-psychology, with its implication that the seat of sacredness lies within the self, misled many Americans into thinking that the inner journey was the most direct path to the sacred expressive life as well as to 'more of everything.'"[29] Any viable social ethic has real work to do—it must bind the individual to society, mesh society's goals with those of the individual, and hold that society together, keeping it from degenerating into a chaos of competing interests.

As spiritual director, one of the roles of the therapist or pastor is to help people develop a social ethic more conducive to self-fulfillment than either self-denial or the belief that one's ultimate responsibility is to oneself. If American culture can develop a persuasive social ethic, perhaps each of us can participate in the larger story of our time, and society can begin to function cohesively. Yankelovich believes that he sees such a movement developing, which he calls "an ethic of commitment." The concept of commitment shifts the emphasis away from both self-denial and self-fulfillment toward connectedness with the natural world, other people, institutions, beliefs, ideas, and experiences. "It discards the Maslowian checklist of inner needs and potentials of the self, and seeks instead the elusive freedom [that Hannah] Arendt describes as the treasure people sometimes discover when they are free to join with others in shaping the tasks and shared meanings of their times."[30]

A new ethic of community requires that we all change our strategies of self-fulfillment, abandoning the assumption that our desires are synonymous with our needs and that the attempt to fulfill these desires is an end in itself. We must realize that the self is more than the sum of its desires, that self-fulfillment demands commitments that endure, and that the sacred can be realized through a web of shared meanings that transcend the isolated self. But this is not all. We must also form commitments that advance the well-being of the community as well as of ourselves. For this to occur, we must coordinate the efforts of our friends and neighbors and of society at large—the leaders of business, religion, education, labor, media, science, and the arts—in an attempt to link our personal aspirations to the comon good of society.

A revived social ethic would preserve such traditional American values as political freedom; the use of that freedom to secure well-being through effort; the comforts and consolations of family life; and pride in America's unique role in history. At the same time it would embrace newer values such as greater autonomy for both men and women; greater tolerance of variant lifestyles; the idea that life is an adventure as well as an economic chore; respect for self-expression and creativity; and a larger place for the awe, mystery, and sacredness of life.

I have argued that our culture's inability to acknowledge death has resulted in large part from the tyrannies of technology and unrestrained individualism. If this thesis is correct, then an ethic of community may bring about a profound change in our response to death. Moving beyond individualism to a sense of social commitment requires great faith. It also calls us to an even greater surrender to the ways in which God's love is manifested in human life. The path of brokenness, of mourning, of remorse leads eventually to both intrapersonal and interpersonal connectedness.

Notes

Chapter 1

1. Quoted in Robert Favre, *La Mort dans la littérature et la pensée françaises au siècle des lumières* (Lyons: Presses Universitaires de Lyon, 1978).

2. Geoffrey Gorer, "The Pornography of Death" in W. Philips and P. Rahv eds., *Modern Writing* (New York: McGraw-Hill, 1956), 56–62.

3. For a representative selection of publications in the field, see Michel Vovelle, "Rediscovery of Death Since 1960," *American Academy of Political and Social Sciences Annals* 447 (January 1980): 89–99. Vovelle's interest is primarily historical. One should also see Martin L. Kutscher, Daniel J. Cherico, Austin H. Kutscher, et al., eds., *A Comprehensive Bibliography of the Thanatology Literature* (New York: Arno Press, 1975), and Robert Fulton, *Death, Grief, and Bereavement: A Bibliography, 1845–1975* (New York: Arno Press, 1976), both of which give primary, though not exclusive, attention to empirically oriented studies.

4. The *New York Times* also reported in that year that in "each year since its paperback publication in 1970, *On Death and Dying* has sold a greater number of copies and has now reached a total of 1,032,000." *The New York Times Book Review*, August 29, 1976, 23.

5. Philippe Ariès, *The Hour of Our Death*, trans. Helen Weaver (New York: Alfred A. Knopf, 1981).

6. Ariès, *Hour*, 603.

7. Ariès, *Hour*, 28. Jankélévitch also suggests this term in *La Mort* (Paris: Flammarion, 1966).

8. Ariès, *Hour*, 138–39.

9. Richard Schulz, *The Psychology of Death, Dying, and Bereavement* (Reading, MA: Addison-Wesley Publishing Co., 1978), 51–52.

10. Bayliss Manning, "Legal and Policy Issues in the Allocation of Death," in Orville G. Brim et al., eds., *The Dying Patient* (New York: Russell Sage Foundation, 1970), 255.

11. Marion Levy, *Modernization: Latecomers and Survivors* (New York: Basic Books, 1972), 46.

12. Arnold Toynbee, ed., *Man's Concern with Death* (St. Louis: McGraw-Hill, 1968), 124.

13. John Hick, *Death and Eternal Life* (New York: Harper and Row, 1976), 93. Hick has outlined three categories of contemporary theological responses: 1) strongly traditional, reaffirming the images of resurrection, judgment, heaven, and hell; 2) moderately traditional, reaffirming the general conception of an after-life modified in the direction of universal salvation; and 3) radical, suppressing the eschatalogical element of Christianity altogether, or presenting it without the affirmation of personal life after death.

14. Jacob Needleman, *A Sense of the Cosmos* (Garden City, NY: Doubleday, 1975), 3.

15. Robert Hendin, *The Age of Sensation* (New York: W. W. Norton, 1975), 13.

16. Ivan Illych, *Medical Nemesis* (New York: Random House, 1976), 174.

17. Daniel Callahan, *The Tyranny of Survival* (New York: Macmillan, 1973), xiv.

18. Illych, *Nemesis*, 203.

19. Robert Jay Lifton, *The Broken Connection* (New York: Simon and Schuster, 1979), 5.

20. For a history of ideas about mortality, see James P. Carse, *Death and Existence* (New York: John Wiley and Sons, 1980) and Jacques Choron, *Death and Western Thought* (New York: Collier, 1963).

21. Lifton, *Connection*, 44. For a sustained and darkly vivid description of the world's death, see Jonathan Schell, *The Fate of the Earth* (New York: Alfred A. Knopf, 1982).

22. Lifton, *Connection*, 18.

23. Vovelle, "Rediscovery of Death," 90.

24. Introduction to *American Academy of Political and Social Science Annals* 447 (January 1980): 1.

25. Richard Huntington and Peter Metcalf, *Celebration of Death: The Anthropology of Mortuary Ritual* (London, New York: Cambridge University Press, 1979), 203–11.

26. Philip Rieff, *The Triumph of the Therapeutic* (New York: Harper and Row, 1966), 205.

27. Rieff, *Triumph*, 391.

28. Callahan, *Tyranny*, 141.

Chapter 2

1. Elisabeth Kübler-Ross, *Death: The Final Stage of Growth* (Englewood Cliffs, N. J.: Prentice-Hall, 1975), xix.

2. Kübler-Ross, *On Death and Dying* (New York: Macmillan, 1969), 26–27.

3. Peter Koestenbaum, *Is There an Answer to Death?* (Englewood Cliffs, N.J.: Prentice-Hall, 1976), 10.

4. Herman Feifel, "The Meaning of Death in American Society," in B. R. Green and D. P. Irish, eds., *Death Education* (Cambridge, Mass.: Schocken, 1973), 12.

5. This indictment is found widely in both popular and scholarly literature. See, for example, John Hinton, *Dying* (London: Penguin, 1967); Daniel McGuire, *Death by Choice* (Cambridge, Mass.: Schocken, 1974); Cicely Saunders, "Dying, They Live: St. Christopher's Hospice," in Herman Feifel, ed., *New Meanings of Death* (New York: McGraw-Hill, 1977), 154–79; and Hans O. Mauksch, "The Organizational Context of Dying," in Elisabeth Kübler-Ross, ed., *Death: The Final Stage of Growth* (Englewood Cliffs, N.J.: Prentice-Hall, 1975), 7–24.

6. Reported in Robert Kastenbaum and Robert Aisenberg, *The Psychology of Death* (New York: Springer, 1972), 53.

7. Among the groups involved in such issues are Concern for Dying and the Society for the Right To Die, both in New York City; the American Society of Law and Medicine, Boston; the Hastings Center, Hastings-on-Hudson, New York; and the Society for Health and Human Values, McLean, Virginia.

8. Ralph H. Turner and Lewis M. Killian, *Collective Behavior* (New York: Houghton Mifflin, 1972), 259.

9. Kübler-Ross, *On Death and Dying*, 5–6.

10. For general discussions of the counterculture, see Theodore Roszak, *The Making of a Counter Culture* (Garden City, N. Y.: Doubleday, 1969) and Lewis Mumford, *The Myth of the Machine* (New York: Harcourt, Brace, and World, 1967–70).

11. Marjorie McCoy, *To Die with Style* (Nashville: Abingdon Press, 1974), 16.

12. Keith Kerr, "Death and Grief Counselling," *Marriage and Family Counselors Quarterly* (Winter 1972): 29–30.

13. Robert Kavanaugh, *Facing Death* (London: Penguin, 1972), 79.

14. David Cole Gordon, *Overcoming the Fear of Death* (New York: Macmillan, 1970), 106, 108–9.

15. Stanislav Grof and John Halifax, *The Human Encounter with Death* (New York: Dutton, 1977).

16. Robert Kastenbaum, *Between Life and Death* (New York: Springer, 1979).

17. John Hinton, *Dying* (London, Penguin, 1967), 64.

18. T. E. Zuehlke and J. T. Watkins, "The Study of Psychotherapy with Dying Patients: An Exploratory Study," *Journal of Clinical Psychology* 31 (1975): 729–32.

19. Rainer Maria Rilke, *The Notebooks of Malte Laurids Bugge*, John Linton, trans., (London: Hogarth Press, 1959), 30.

20. Kübler-Ross, *On Death and Dying*.

21. Quoted in Loma Feigenberg, *Terminal Care: Terminal Friendship Contracts* (New York: Brunner/Mazel, 1978), 48.

22. Michael Simpson, "Social and Psychological Aspects of Dying," in Hannelore Wass, ed., *Dying* (New York: McGraw-Hill, 1979), 124.

23. Stanley Keleman, *Living Your Dying* (New York: Random, 1974), 4.

24. Schneidman, *Voices of Death* (New York: Harper and Row, 1980), 111–12.

25. Avery D. Weisman, "The Right Way to Die," *Psychiatric and Social Service Review* 2 (1968): 3.

26. Avery D. Weisman, *On Dying and Denying* (New York: Behavioral Publications, 1972), 33.

27. Lisl M. Goodman, *Death and the Creative Life* (New York: Springer, 1981).

28. "Specialist on Dying Says People Don't," October 16, 1975, p. 23.

29. Raymond Moody, *Life after Life* (New York: Bantam, 1975) and *Reflections on Life after Life* (New York: Bantam, 1977).

30. I. Stevenson, "Research into the Evidence of Man's Survival after Death," *Journal of Nervous and Mental Disease* 165 (1977): 152–70.

31. Robert Kastenbaum, "Temptations from the Afterlife," *Human Behavior* (September 1977): 28–33.

Chapter 3

1. See the work of B. F. Skinner: "The Operational Analysis of Psychological Terms," *Psychological Review* 52 (1945): 270–77; *Science and Human Behavior* (New York: Macmillan, 1953); *Verbal Behavior* (New York: Appleton-Century-Crofts, 1958); and *About Behaviorism* (New York: Knopf, 1974).

2. William Barrett, *The Illusion of Technique* (Garden City: Doubleday, 1979), 210.

3. Charles Tart, ed., *Altered States of Consciousness: A Book of Readings* (New York: Wiley, 1969); *States of Consciousness* (New York: Dutton, 1975); *Transpersonal Psychologies* (New York: Harper and Row, 1975); *Psi: Scientific Studies of the Psychic Realm* (New York: Dutton, 1977).

4. See R. S. Valle and M. King, eds., *Existential-Phenomenological Alternatives in Psychology* (New York: Oxford University Press, 1978).

5. Sigmund Freud, "Inhibitions, Symptoms, and Anxiety," *Standard Edition of the Complete Works of Sigmund Freud*, vol. 20 (London: Hogarth, 1953), 130.

6. Freud, "Thoughts for the Times on War and Death," *Complete Works* 14, 289.

7. Freud, "Inhibitions," 130.

8. Freud, "War and Death," 297.

9. However, Robert Jay Lifton cites evidence that depth psychology is beginning to move in the opposite direction, increasingly seeing castration anxiety as a manifestation of death anxiety, rather than the reverse (*Broken Connection*, 49).

10. Freud, "War and Death," 299–300.

11. Gregory Zilboorg, "Fear of Death," *Psychoanalytic Quarterly* 12 (1943): 465.

12. Kurt R. Eissler, *The Psychiatrist and the Dying Patient* (New York: International Universities Press, 1955), 25.

13. Maurice Merleau-Ponty, *Phenomenology of Perception* (London: Routledge and Kegan Paul, 1962); *The Structure of Behavior* (Boston: Beacon Press, 1963); *The Visible and the Invisible* (Evanston, Ill.: Northwestern University Press, 1968); and *Themes from the Lectures* (Evanston, Ill.: Northwestern University Press, 1970).

14. Médard Boss, *Meaning and Content of Sexual Perversions: A Daseinanalytical Approach to the Psychopathology of the Phenomenon of Love* (New York: Grune and Stratton, 1949), 46.

15. Merleau-Ponty, *Perception*, 32.

16. Ernest Becker, *The Denial of Death* (New York: Free Press, 1973), 164ff.

17. Becker, *Denial*, 166.

18. Becker, *Denial*, 217.

19. Becker, *Denial*, 98.

20. Ibid.

21. Ibid.

22. Lifton, *Connection*, 51–52.

23. Lucy Bregman, "Three Psycho-Mythologies of Death: Becker, Hillman, and Lifton." Paper delivered at the American Academy of Religion, New York, December 1982,

24. Becker, *Denial*, 30–35.

25. Some practitioners of related therapies appear to have reverted to an obsession with and glorification of the physical body, an approach that implies that the body is the deepest reality, rather than what it is—simply the lowest of all modes of consciousness. It is the *integration* of body and ego that constitutes the deepest reality.

26. Keleman, *Living*, 72–74.

27. Keleman, *Living*, 81.

28. Keleman, *Living*, 127.

29. Keleman, *Living*, 129.

30. Keleman, *Living*, 151.

31. Keleman, *Living*, 156.

32. Koestenbaum, *Answer*, 50.

33. Koestenbaum, *Answer*, 7.

34. Koestenbaum, *Answer*, 11.

35. Koestenbaum, *Answer*, 50.

36. Koestenbaum, *Answer*, 53

37. Koestenbaum, *Answer*, 165.

38. C. G. Jung, "The Archetypes and the Collective Unconscious," *Collected Works*, vol. 9, part 1 (Princeton: Bollingen Series 20, 1968), 190.

39. Ken Wilbur, *No Boundary* (Los Angeles: Center Publications, 1979), 126.

40. Edgar Herzog, *Psyche and Death* (New York: Putnam, 1967), 9.

41. Herzog, *Psyche*, 10.

42. Herzog, *Psyche*, 15–17.

43. Herzog, *Psyche*, 135.

44. Herzog, *Psyche*, 27.

45. Gail Sheehy, *Passages* (New York: Bantam, 1977).

46. Robert Ornstein, *The Psychology of Consciousness* (San Francisco: Freeman, 1972), 96–99.

47. John Eccles, *The Human Psyche* (New York: Springer International, 1980), ix.

48. John J. Crook, *The Evolution of Human Consciousness* (New York: Oxford University Press, 1980), viii.

49. Crook, *Human Consciousness*, 353.

Chapter 4

1. For an extensive discussion of the relationship between psychiatry and the sacred, see Jacob Needleman and Dennis Lewis, eds., *On the Way to Self-Knowledge* (New York: Knopf, 1976).

2. Needleman, *Cosmos*, 112.

3. Abraham Maslow, *Religions, Values, and Peak-Experiences* (New York: Viking, 1970), 95.

4. Maslow, *The Farther Reaches of Human Nature* (New York: Viking, 1971), 33.

5. Maslow, *Peak-Experiences*, 22ff.

6. Claudio Naranjo, *The One Quest* (New York: Ballantine, 1972), 10.

7. Lucy Bregman, *The Rediscovery of Inner Experience* (Chicago: Nelson-Hall, 1982), vii.

8. For a full discussion of the concept of hierophany, see Mircea Eliade, *Patterns in Comparative Religion* (Cleveland: World, 1967).

9. Cited by Bregman, *Inner Experience*, 4.

10. Edwin Schur, *The Awareness Trap: Self-Absorption Instead of Social Change* (New York: McGraw-Hill, 1977); Russell Jacoby, *Social Amnesia: A Critique of Contemporary Psychology from Adler to Laing* (Boston: Beacon, 1975).

11. Avery Weisman, *On Dying and Denial* (New York: Behavioral Publications, 1972), 112.

12. Lifton, *Connection*, 17.

13. Lifton, *Connection*, 8.

14. Lifton, *Connection*, 339.

15. Lifton, *Connection*, 369.

16. Lifton, *Connection*, 392.

17. Needleman, *Cosmos*, 112.

18. Needleman, *Cosmos*, 162.

19. Needleman, *Cosmos*, 58.

20. Needleman, *Cosmos*, 61.

21. W. Wentz-Evans, *The Tibetan Book of the Dead* (London: Oxford Press, 1968). Especially instructive is the introduction by C. G. Jung.

22. Needleman, *Cosmos*, 62.

23. Quoted by Eugene L. Stockwell, "The Greatest Missionary Challenge of Our Day?," *World Encounter* (Fall 1984), 19.

24. Vladimir Lossky, *The Mystical Theology of the Eastern Church* (Attic, 1957), 9, 39.

25. Paul Tillich, *The Courage to Be* (New Haven: Yale University Press, 1952), 32ff.

26. Thomas Merton, *Contemplative Prayer* (New York: Image Books, 1971), 29.

27. Anthony the Great, *The Letters of St. Anthony*, trans. Derwas Chitty (London: SLG Press, 1979), 352.

28. C. F. Kelley, *Meister Eckhart on Divine Knowledge* (New Haven: Yale University Press, 1977), 139.

29. *The Cloud of Unknowing* (London: Burns, Oates, and Washbourne, 1940), 80.

30. Richard P. Handy, *Search for Nothing: The Life of St. John of the Cross* (New York: Crossroads, 1982), 88.

31. St. Teresa of Avila, *The Interior Castle* (New York: Paulist Press, 1979), 25.

32. Jaroslav Pelikan, *The Shape of Death* (Nashville: Abingdon, 1961).

33. William Stringfellow, *A Simplicity of Faith: My Experience in Mourning* (Nashville: Abingdon, 1982), 39.

Chapter 5

1. For an extended discussion and analysis of representative theologians, see Milton McGatch, *Death: Meaning and Mortality in Christian Thought and Contemporary Culture* (New York: Seabury, 1969).

2. Discussions of the pertinent thought of representative theologians and philosophers may be found in James B. Carse, *Death and Existence: A Conceptual History of Human Mortality* (New York: Wiley, 1980) and Jacques Choron, *Death and Western Thought* (New York: Collier, 1963).

3. See representative essays in John Donnelly, ed., *Language, Metaphysics, and Death* (New York: Fordham University Press, 1978).

4. Josef Pieper, *Death and Immortality*, trans. R. S. C. Winston (New York: Fordham University Press, 1969), 12, 17.

5. Pieper, *Death and Immortality*, 35ff.

6. Pieper, *Death and Immortality*, 32, 36–46.

7. Pieper, *Death and Immortality*, 72.

8. Pieper, *Death and Immortality*, 37.

9. Karl Rahner, "Ideas for a Theology of Death," *Theological Investigations*, vol. 13 (Baltimore: Helicon, 1975), 17.

10. Rahner, "Theology of Death," 179.

11. Robert E. Neale, *The Art of Dying* (New York: Harper and Row, 1973).

12. Neale, *Art of Dying*, 42–43.

13. Neale, *Art of Dying*, 85, 90.

14. Roger Troisfontaines, *I Do Not Die* (New York: Crossroads, 1963).

15. Troisfontaines, *I Do Not Die*, 133.

16. Troisfontaines, *I Do Not Die*, 135.

17. Troisfontaines, *I Do Not Die*, 140.

18. Troisfontaines, *I Do Not Die*, 146.

19. Ladislaus Boros, *The Mystery of Death* (New York: Seabury, 1965); see also "Death: A Theological Reflection," in Michael J. Taylor, ed., *The Mystery of Suffering and Death* (New York: Image Books, 1974).

20. Boros, *Mystery*, 31–47.

21. Boros, *Mystery*, 35.

22. Boros, *Mystery*, 152–53.

23. Rahner, "Theology of Death," 40.

24. Rahner, "Theology of Death," 41, 55.

25. Rahner, "Theology of Death," 31.

26. Rahner, "Theology of Death," 32.

27. Rahner, "Theology of Death," 111. See also "On Christian Dying," *Theological Investigations*, vol. 7 (Baltimore: Helicon Press, 1972), 288.

28. Elie Wiesel, quoted in Samuel J. Freedman, "Bearing Witness: The Life and Work of Elie Wiesel," *The New York Times Magazine* (October 23, 1983), 36.

29. Daniel Yankelovich, *New Rules: Searching for Self-Fulfillment in a World Turned Upside Down* (New York: Random, 1981), 245.

30. Yankelovich, *New Rules*, 245. See also Hannah Arendt, *On Revolution* (New York: Viking, 1963), 28.

Index